MODERN HUMANITIES RESEARCH ASSOCIATION
CRITICAL TEXTS
VOLUME 41

La Tina
Equivoci rusticali

by
Antonio Malatesti

Edited by
Davide Messina

Modern Humanities Research Association

2014

Published by

The Modern Humanities Research Association,
1 Carlton House Terrace
London SW1Y 5AF
United Kingdom

© *The Modern Humanities Research Association, 2014*

First published 2014

ISBN 978-1-78188-052-4

Copies may be ordered from www.criticaltexts.mhra.org.uk

CONTENTS

ACKNOWLEDGEMENTS

I have learned a lot during the research for this little volume. For their generous help, discerning advice, and invaluable patience, I would like to thank: Professor Peter Brand, Professor Alastair Fowler, and in particular Professor Brian Richardson, Italian Editor of the Critical Texts series; Gerard Lowe, MHRA Publishing Manager; the staff of the National Library of Scotland, and in particular Chris Taylor, International Collections Manager; the staff of the Advocates Library, Edinburgh, and in particular Lindsay Levy, Rare Books Cataloguer; the staff of the Biblioteca Nazionale Centrale di Firenze, Sala Manoscritti, and the staff of the other main Florentine libraries: Riccardiana, Moreniana, and Medicea Laurenziana; the staff of the Accademia della Crusca, Archivio Storico, and in particular Dottoressa Elisabetta Benucci; the staff of the Biblioteca dell'Archiginnasio, Bologna; Dottoressa Paola Mario of the Biblioteca dell'Orto Botanico, University of Padua; Dottoressa Silvana Naccarato, Director of the Biblioteca Civica di Cosenza; last but not least, the University of Edinburgh, in particular for the research leave that allowed me to complete the Introduction. For all the names not mentioned here, there is a bigger book where they will never be forgotten: thank you.

ABBREVIATIONS

The following abbreviations are used in this volume:

BML   Biblioteca Medicea Laurenziana, Florence
BNCF   Biblioteca Nazionale Centrale, Florence
BR   Biblioteca Riccardiana, Florence
CDL   Jean Toscan, *Le Carnaval du langage: le lexique érotique des poètes de l'équivoque de Burchiello à Marino (XVᵉ-XVIIᵉ siècles)*, 4 vols (Lille: Presses Universitaires, 1981)
CHIL   *The Cambridge History of Italian Literature*, ed. by Peter Brand and Lino Pertile (Cambridge: Cambridge University Press, 1996)
CPW   *Complete Prose Works of John Milton*, ed. by Don M. Wolfe and others, 8 vols (New Haven: Yale University Press, 1953–82)
DBI   *Dizionario biografico degli italiani*, dir. by Alberto M. Ghisalberti and others (Rome: Istituto della Enciclopedia Italiana Treccani, 1960– in progress)
NLS   National Library of Scotland, Edinburgh

INTRODUCTION

~

I have known rustic revels in my youth.[1]

The Florentine poet Antonio Malatesti (1610–1672) merits a brief mention in the first *Storia della letteratura italiana*, compiled by the Jesuit bibliographer Girolamo Tiraboschi, for his original contributions to the renewal of the sonnet form in two particular genres of the Tuscan tradition: enigmatography, with his popular collection of riddles entitled *La Sfinge*, first published in 1640; and dithyrambic poetry, with his *Brindisi de' Ciclopi*, first published posthumously in 1673.[2] In more recent times, however, his name crops up most frequently in early modern English studies, because of a sequence of fifty equivocal sonnets in the rustic style entitled *La Tina* (1637), which Malatesti dedicated and presented to John Milton on the occasion of his visit to Florence in 1638. The dedicated manuscript has elicited the curiosity of many scholars, but its very existence has also been disputed. The present edition is based on the rediscovery of the original autograph manuscript,[3] and aims to contribute to a wider understanding of Malatesti's minor but exemplary position in the history of seventeenth-century Italian literature.

1. Malatesti: Portrait of an Ingenious Gentleman

In the celebrated mock-heroic poem *Il Malmantile racquistato*, composed by the poet and painter Lorenzo Lippi (1606–1665) under the anagrammatic pseudonym of Perlone Zipoli, the sixty-first stanza of the first cantare makes a swift but salient portrait of General 'Amostante Laton, poeta insigne', who leads

---

[1] George Meredith, *Modern Love and Poems of the English Roadside, with Poems and Ballads* (London: Chapman & Hall, 1862); now ed. by Rebecca N. Mitchell and Criscilla Benford (New Haven and London: Yale University Press, 2012), p. 40.

[2] Girolamo Tiraboschi, *Storia della letteratura italiana*, 16 vols (Modena: Società tipografica, 1772–1782), VIII (1780), p. 310. See Antonio Malatesti, *Brindis* [sic] *de Ciclopi* (Florence: Stamperia della Stella, 1673), and *La Sfinge: enimmi* (Venice: Sarzina, 1640). On Malatesti, see Girolamo De Miranda's entry in *DBI*, 68 (2007), pp. 114–16.

[3] See Davide Messina, '*La Tina* Regained', *Milton Quarterly*, 45 (2011), 118–22. See also Edward Jones, 'The Archival Landscape of Milton's Youth, University Years, and Pre-London Residencies', in *Young Milton: The Emerging Author, 1620–1642*, ed. by Edward Jones (Oxford: Oxford University Press, 2013), pp. 3–20 (p. 4).

the reconquest of the old castle of Malmantile, near Florence, and eventually marries the legitimate queen.[4] The General is described as 'matto' and 'spolpato', that is to say as 'mad' and 'lean-bodied' as we imagine Don Quixote, whose adventures had been recently translated into Italian by the Florentine Lorenzo Franciosini.[5] The name of this Quixotesque character is but an anagram of Antonio Malatesti, who also wrote the summary octaves heading each cantare;[6] one line summarizes his main exploits and achievements: 'Stampa gli Enigmi, strolaga e dipigne' (I. 61. 4).

Malatesti studied painting with Lippi, who also made his portrait and that of his mistress.[7] We do not have knowledge of any particular painting by Malatesti, but we do know that his drawing skills were equally instrumental in the study of astrology, which he cultivated in the spirit of a genuine amateur. It is worth noting that astrology should not be simply understood as the casting of horoscopes: his mentor was Ludovico Serenai, the closest disciple of the physicist Evangelista Torricelli, who succeeded Galileo Galilei as court mathematician in Florence.[8]

More than an amateur painter and astrologer, at any rate, Malatesti was a prolific and ingenious poet, with a real flair for enigmatography. In the second edition of La Sfinge, published in 1641 with a few changes, the fifth riddle, 'Con la spoglia dorata ecco un Serpente', was on the telescope donated by Galileo to the Grand Duke Cosimo II — 'senza tosco, un gran Tosco, al Re de' Toschi'.[9]

---

[4] Lorenzo Lippi, *Il Malmantile racquistato: poema di Perlone Zipoli*, ed. by Giovanni Cinelli Calvoli (Finaro [Florence]: Rossi, 1676); commented edn *Il Malmantile racquistato di Perlone Zipoli, con le note di Puccio Lamoni* [Paolo Minucci], ed. by Anton Maria Biscioni, 2 vols (Florence: Moücke, 1750), I, 92.

[5] See Miguel de Cervantes, *L'ingegnoso cittadino Don Chisciotte della Mancia*, trans. by Lorenzo Franciosini, 2 vols (Venice: Baba, 1622–25).

[6] See *Argomenti fatti dal Malatesti al Poema del Lippi*, BNCF, MS Magl. VII. 392, fols 106ʳ–11ʳ; cf. MS Magl. VII. 391, fol. 247.

[7] Lippi's portraits are now lost or as yet unidentified, but we have a number of sonnets by Malatesti addressed to Lippi, in which the paintings are mentioned: see Arnaldo Alterocca, *La vita e l'opera poetica e pittorica di Lorenzo Lippi: con nuove indagini e rime inedite* (Catania: Battiato, 1914), pp. 124–26, 210–22. See also Chiara D'Afflitto, *Lorenzo Lippi* (Florence: Edifir, 2002), p. 94, n. 98; cf. *Ritratto di pittore* (c. 1630), p. 215, and *Ritratto virile di profilo* (c. 1647–48), p. 279.

[8] On Serenai and Torricelli, see Fabio Toscan, *L'erede di Galileo: vita breve e mirabile di Evangelista Torricelli* (Milan: Sironi, 2008), p. 91. Cf. Filippo Baldinucci, *Notizie de' professori del disegno da Cimabue in qua*, 6 vols (Florence: Stamperia di S.A.R., 1681–1728), VI: *Secolo V, dal 1610 al 1670* (1728), p. 566. Lippi emphasizes that Amostante-Malatesti 'sa d'astrologia' (p. 148, III. 35. 6). See Robert S. Westman, 'The Astronomer's Role in the Sixteenth Century: A Preliminary Study', *History of Science*, 18 (1980), 105–47. Cf. Antonio Favaro, 'Galileo astrologo, secondo i documenti editi e inediti', *Mente e Cuore*, 8 (1881), 99–108.

[9] *La Sfinge: enimmi di Antonio Malatesti. Con aggiunta La Tina*, ed. by Ettore Allodoli (Lanciano: Carabba, 1913), p. 21 (l. 14). Cf. Nunzio Vaccaluzzo, *Galileo Galilei nella poesia del suo secolo* (Milan: Sandron, 1910), p. 51.

The great astronomer liked it so much that he replied *per le rime*, namely with a meta-enigmatic sonnet on the definition of the riddle, which Malatesti later proudly prefaced to the third edition in 1643.[10] A posthumous fourth edition of *La Sfinge* was brought out in 1683, in three parts, enriched with a number of quatrains on the Florentine card game called *minchiate*. One of the new riddles, 'Astolfo vantator, Namo prestante', is an enigmatographic self-portrait of Malatesti: his first name can be derived from the initials of the seven Carolingian knights listed in the first quatrain, while his last name is encrypted in the last line, where the poet is described as 'un ch'à infer*ma la testa* il cervel sano'.[11]

The reference to chivalric poetry in the opening acronym of this self-portrait may also be read in the light of Malatesti's noteworthy first poetic work, written when he was still in his teens: the *Rinaldo infuriato*, a heroic poem in ten cantos dedicated to the Grand Duke Ferdinand II, of the same age as Malatesti, and prefaced by the lawyer and poet Jacopo Cicognini (1577–1633), who encouraged the young poet to complete the work.[12] The connection with the Cicogninis was meaningful in many ways for the poetic apprenticeship of Malatesti, who always remained 'allegro compagno alla vita scapata' of Jacopo's son, the talented playwright Giacinto Andrea (1606–1649);[13] when Jacopo died, the twenty-three-year-old Malatesti published a commemorative sonnet together with Gabriello Chiabrera,[14] the most influential Tuscan poet of the seventeenth century, who also initiated the revival of dithyrambic poetry 'all'uso dei Greci' with his *Vendemmie di Parnaso*.[15] Disappointingly, the first three cantos of Malatesti's youthful poem were only published in 1782 by Modesto Rastrelli, in a collection of *Poesie piacevoli e burlesche* which were at once seized and pulped because they

---

[10] Malatesti was pleased to note: 'Il Signor Galileo Galilei, avendo letta la prima parte de' miei Enimmi, non isdegnò di abbassar la sua famosa penna con la piacevolezza del verso, mandandomi il presente sonetto con esortarmi a far la seconda parte' (*La Sfinge*, p. 18). Cf. Galileo Galilei, *Opere*, ed. by Antonio Favaro, 20 vols (Florence: Barbèra, 1890–1909), IX: *Scritti letterari* (1899), pp. 26 and 227.

[11] *La Sfinge*, p. 134 (my italics).

[12] See BNCF, MS Naz. II. IV. 238 (ex-Magl. VII. 229); Cicognini's preface is at fols 3–5.

[13] See Mario Sterzi, 'Jacopo Cicognini', *Giornale storico e letterario della Liguria*, 3 (1902), 289–338 (p. 299).

[14] The two sonnets were published in the first edition of Cicognini's *Trionfo di David* (Florence: Zanobi Pignoni, 1633), which had been staged in 1629 with scene painting by Lippi (see D'Afflitto, pp. 30, and 75). Cf. *Raccolta di poesie*, BNCF, MS Magl. VII. 357, fol. 122ʳ.

[15] Gabriello Chiabrera, *Vendemmie di Parnaso*, in *Rime: parte prima* (Venice: Combi, 1605); now in *Canzonette, Rime varie, Dialoghi*, ed. by Luigi Negri (Turin: UTET, 1964), pp. 217–57; this work includes a poem addressed 'Al Signor Iacopo Cicognini, con promessa di buoni vini' (pp. 243–44). Cicognini also featured in Chiabrera's dialogue *L'Orzalesi, ovvero della tessitura delle canzoni*, ibid., pp. 541–60.

contained 'cose contrarie alla religione', having received the censors' licence by apparent mistake.[16]

The *Rinaldo infuriato* was conceived as a sequel to the famous *Orlando furioso* by Ludovico Ariosto, perhaps following the *Rinaldo ardito* attributed to 'un Ludovico Ariosto' by the (often unreliable) Florentine polygraph Anton Francesco Doni;[17] but it is also possible that the young Malatesti wanted to rival Torquato Tasso, who had composed a *Rinaldo* in twelve cantos when he was just eighteen years old.[18] In addition to Ariosto and Tasso, as emphasized by Cicognini, Malatesti owed much of his linguistic invention to another founding masterpiece in the Italian epic genre, the *Morgante* by Luigi Pulci, where we also find 'l'ardito Rinaldo'.[19] This is significant, among other reasons, because Pulci's work was based on the fourteenth-century poem *La Spagna*:[20] it was precisely the Spanish dramatic tradition that was coming to the foreground at the end of the Renaissance, beginning with the *Comedia Tinelaria* (*c.* 1516) by Bartolomé de Torres Naharro, first performed in Rome for the Medici Pope Leo X.[21] Among what Vincenzo Viviani termed his 'pochissimi libri',[22] even Galileo had a copy of Franciosini's translation of *Don Quixote*, in which Rinaldo's helmet is parodied

[16] *Poesie piacevoli e burlesche per divertimento, e passatempo, di vari eccellenti autori*, ed. by Modesto Rastrelli (Yverdon [Florence: Benucci], 1782); canto I is in vol. III (pp. 74–96), cantos II–III in vol. IV, which also includes a *Lettera di Modesto Rastrelli compilatore a Antonio Malatesti* and several other poems by Malatesti. Cf. Costantino Arlìa, 'Un libro ignoto a' bibliografi', *Il Bibliofilo: Giornale dell'arte antica e moderna*, 5 (1885), 74–76 (p. 76). On Rastrelli, see Maria A. Morelli Timpanaro, *Autori, stampatori, librai: per una storia dell'editoria a Firenze nel secolo XVIII* (Florence: Olschki, 1999), pp. 358–65 and 422–25.
[17] Anton F. Doni, *Seconda libraria* (Venice: Marcolini, 1551), p. 82. Cf. Michele Catalano, *Vita di Ludovico Ariosto, ricostruita su nuovi documenti*, 2 vols (Geneva: Olschki, 1930–31), I (1930), pp. 278–79.
[18] Torquato Tasso, *Rinaldo: edizione critica basata sulla seconda edizione del 1570 con le varianti della princeps (1562)*, ed. by Michael Sherberg (Ravenna: Longo, 1990). Cf. Charles P. Brand, *Torquato Tasso: A Study of the Poet and of his Contribution to English Poetry* (Cambridge: Cambridge University Press, 1965), pp. 63 and 67.
[19] Luigi Pulci, *Il Morgante Maggiore*, ed. by Pietro Sermolli, 2 vols (Florence: Le Monnier, 1855), I, 171 (IX. 57. 8).
[20] See *La Spagna*, ed. by M. Catalano, 3 vols (Bologna: Commissione per i testi di lingua, 1939–40).
[21] Bartolomé de Torres Naharro, *Comedia Tinellaria*, in *'Propalladia' and Other Works*, ed. by Joseph E. Gillet, 4 vols (Bryn Mawr, PA: 1943–1961), II: *Collected Plays* (Menasha, WI: Banta, 1946), 187–267. Cf. Luisa de Aliprandini, 'La Tinellaria nella cultura italiana del primo Cinquecento', in Bartolomé de Torres Naharro, *Comedia Tinelaria* (Bologna: Forni, 1985), pp. 5–73.
[22] Vincenzo Viviani, *Racconto istorico della vita di Galileo* (1654), in Galilei, *Opere*, XIX (1907), 597–632 (p. 625). Cf. Antonio Favaro, *La libreria di Galileo Galilei descritta e illustrata* (Rome: Tipografia delle Scienze Matematiche e Fisiche, 1887), p. 7. See also Crystal Hall, *Galileo's Reading* (Cambridge: Cambridge University Press, 2013).

with a barber's basin.[23] It is on this new cultural stage that we see a close parallel between the dramatic talent of Giacinto Cicognini, who composed many popular works in the Spanish style, and the development of rustic poetry,[24] which highlights elements of continuity within the Tuscan tradition towards the eighteenth-century pastoral drama.

As well as nurturing his aspirations in the heroic genre, the young Malatesti was soon employed in the silk trade. The 'Arte della Seta' was one of the major guilds in Florence, but the young poet exhausted his profits in gambling and devoted considerable effort to the pursuit of other expensive and less chivalrous adventures, with a growing sense of frustration, as Rastrelli commented: 'La passione che predominava il nostro poeta era la Poesia, ma più della poesia il bel Sesso: or senza denaro si tentano invano le avventure del Regno Amoroso'.[25] He then retired to his modest family villa in Taiano, on the south-eastern hillsides of Florence called 'l'Apparita'. Here, he indulged in the poetic genres that were more congenial to his ebullient spirit and could divert him from his impecunious and reclusive country life, as recounted in an epistolary poem addressed to Lippi: 'se ho a lavorar senza speranza | Di guadagno, vo' pur fare il Poeta'.[26]

For his services to the princes Don Lorenzo and Mattias de' Medici, who often commissioned festive songs and celebratory verses, Ferdinand II finally endowed Malatesti with a comfortable post at the 'Ufficio del Sale'. We still have many of his poems penned on the back of the salt-tax receipts. A stanza of *Il Malmantile*, probably authored by Malatesti himself, playfully alludes to his lifelong post commenting that a witty blend of 'sale e inchiostro in salamoia' will preserve *La Sfinge* from oblivion (VIII. 26); his book of riddles is in fact listed among the bizarre and marvellous objects in the 'Galleria delle Fate', where we also find Don Quixote's lance (VIII. 33).

---

[23] Pierpaolo Antonello aptly commented: 'Galileo chiude ad un tempo il Cinquecento e apre le porte alla modernità, senza però riuscire a farne compiutamente parte, ancorché sullo scaffale della sua biblioteca risuoni rumorosa la risata ironica del *Chisciotte*' ('Galileo scrittore e la critica: Analisi stilistica e interdisciplinarietà', *Quaderni d'italianistica*, 23 (2002), 25–48 (p. 45–46)). For the poetic influence of the Florentine burlesque tradition on Cervantes, see Adrienne Laskier Martín, *Cervantes and the Burlesque Sonnet* (Berkeley-Los Angeles: University of California Press, 1991).

[24] See Joseph E. Gillet, 'Notes on the Language of the Rustics in the Drama of the Sixteenth Century', in *Homenaje ofrecido a Menéndez Pidal*, 3 vols (Madrid: Hernando, 1925), I, 443–53.

[25] Antonio Malatesti, *Enimmi, ossieno Indovinelli piacevoli e galanti, finora inediti*, ed. by M. Rastrelli (Florence: Benucci e Compp., 1782), p. 7.

[26] Antonio Malatesti, *Lettera familiare a Lorenzo Lippi, descrivendogli la sua vita*, ed. by Giulio Piccini (Florence: Cellini e C., 1867), p. 8. Malatesti's family villa is not to be confused with the homonymous 'Villa l'Apparita', as Allodoli explains: 'L'Apparita è una collina sopra Firenze, dalla parte del Bagno a Ripoli, così detta perché da essa appare al viandante il panorama della città' (*La Sfinge*, p. v).

Malatesti's pride lived up to his wit, as he was 'probably the only man in Italy who acquired enduring fame through his riddles', as Michele De Filippis stated in his thorough study of the genre.[27] His family tomb was in the Basilica of Santa Croce, where some of the most notable Florentine poets and artists were buried. It was not only because of his riddles, however, that he unexpectedly won the posthumous fame that 'trae dal sepolcro, e in vita serba', as foreshadowed in the ode to *La Sfinge* by the young classicist Valerio Chimentelli (1620–1668).[28] His name acquired an additional claim to fame with *La Tina*, yet again, not as much for its ingenuous *contaminatio* of the sonnet as for what appeared to be a tongue-in-cheek dedication to the young Milton, and not least because the dedicated manuscript has remained incredibly elusive throughout the centuries.

As soon as Malatesti died, some of his notebooks were held to be 'contra i buoni costumi' and burned,[29] while several others were destroyed by a begrudging bookseller who could not get hold of the poet's library.[30] Fortunately, Malatesti's friend Antonio Magliabechi, court librarian of the Medici-Palatine Library in the Pitti palace, looked after the substantial collection of his extant manuscripts, which are now kept for the most part in the National Library of Florence. As for *La Tina*, the manuscript was dispatched to 'Bertagna che fu poi detta Inghilterra', like Rinaldo in Ariosto's poem, and 'sopra la Scozia ultimamente sorse':[31] it is an intriguing story.

2. Malatesti and Milton: No Passion Spent?

In the summer of 1638, the thirty-year-old Milton arrived in Florence.[32] At that time he had only written a number of 'minor' poems in Latin, Greek, English, and Italian, all of them in the 'easy, vulgar, and therefore disgusting' pastoral style,

---

[27] Michele De Filippis, 'Antonio Malatesti', in *The Literary Riddle in Italy in the Seventeenth Century* (Berkeley and Los Angeles: University of California Press, 1953), pp. 116–48 (p. 117).
[28] *La Sfinge*, p. xxxvi.
[29] See below, Giuseppe Baretti, *Notizie intorno all'Autore*.
[30] In March 1672, the poet Agostino Nelli wrote that 'si erano venduti i libri del S.re Antonio Malatesti' (*Diario di Agostino Nelli dall'anno 1667 fino al 1684*, II, fol. 221). Anton Maria Biscioni reported on Malatesti's library: 'Lasciò novero grande di scritti, ma perché un libraio voleva con le sue cabale porvi sopra le mani, come fece in buona parte de' libri d'un altro, messo in picca studiosamente un gran personaggio con un luogo autorevole, e perché v'erano alcune composizioni, furori della gioventù, tanto quanto pinse, che con poco decoro del Poeta furono studiosamente distrutte, e questo per non poter egli aver suo intento. Ma a dispetto del livore, le migliori sono in mano d'amico carissimo [i.e. Magliabechi], ed un giorno vedransi in luce con somma lode dell'Autore' (*Giunte alla Toscana Letteratura del Cinelli: scrittori fiorentini*, II, BNCF, MS Magl. IX. 70, fols 271ᵛ–72ʳ, pp. 1278–79).
[31] Ludovico Ariosto, *Orlando furioso, secondo la princeps del 1516*, ed. by Marco Dorigatti (Florence: Olschki, 2006), pp. 34 (II. 26. 4) and 80 (IV. 51. 5).
[32] See *The Life Records of John Milton*, ed. by Joseph M. French, 5 vols (New Brunswick, NJ:

as Dr Johnson later deprecated.[33] His Puritan masque popularly known as *Comus*, written in 1634 and printed in 1637, was much praised and sent as a representative work to Sir Henry Wotton, who had been a diplomat in Florence and advised the young poet on his Italian journey; it is unlikely, however, that this work was known in Florence, and the same should be assumed for all of Milton's early English verses, including his recent elegy *Lycidas* (1638), which concludes with a hint at the imminent journey by setting out for 'Pastures new'.[34]

Despite the fact that he was a relatively obscure foreign poet, Milton soon made his way into the main literary circles of Florence and other Italian cities. In an autobiographical passage of *The Reason of Church-Government* (1642), he remembered that in some of the many 'privat academies of *Italy*' he had recited a number of his early poems, probably Latin elegies and Italian sonnets, as a 'proof of his wit', and proudly mentioned that he had received several 'written Encomiums' from his fellow academicians.[35] Five of these *testimonia* were later published in the 1645 edition of his *Minor Poems*, including those of two Florentine academicians, Carlo Roberto Dati and Giovanni Antonio Francini.[36]

Dati and Francini are mentioned in Milton's *Epitaphium Damonis* (1639) as the two friends who made his name known in Italy, along with other 'Pastores Thusci' who donated him books and manuscripts as rustic gifts — 'Fiscellæ, calathique & cerea vincla cicutæ'.[37] They both appear in Lippi's *Malmantile* under the anagrammatic names, respectively, of Alticardo and Franconio Ingannavini. Francini must have reminisced Milton's visit to Florence when, from Paris, he

Rutgers University Press, 1949–58), I: 1608–39 (1949), 371; V: 1670–74 (1958), 385. Cf. Gordon Campbell, *A Milton Chronology* (London: Macmillan, 1997), pp. 60–62, 65–66. On Milton in Florence, see John Arthos, *Milton and the Italian Cities* (London: Bowes and Bowes, 1968), pp. 1–51; Piero Rebora, 'Milton a Firenze', *Nuova antologia*, 88 (1953), now in *Interpretazioni anglo-italiane: saggi e ricerche* (Bari: Adriatica, 1961), pp. 139–57.

[33] Samuel Johnson, *The Lives of the Most Eminent English Poets, with Critical Observations on their Works* (1779–81), ed. by Roger Lonsdale, 4 vols (Oxford: Clarendon Press, 2006), I, 278. Cf. Christine Rees, *Johnson's Milton* (Cambridge: Cambridge University Press, 2010), p. 163; see also Barbara K. Lewalski, 'Genre', in *A Companion to Milton*, ed. by Thomas Corns (Oxford: Blackwell Publishing, 2003), pp. 3–21.

[34] See *The Works of John Milton*, I: *Minor Poems*, ed. by Frank Allen Patterson and others (New York: Columbia University Press, 1931), 76–123 (l. 193). It was Milton's dear friend Charles Diodati, whose family was originally from Lucca, who introduced him to Wotton and to his cousin in Paris Eli Diodati, a good friend of Galileo's: see Donald C. Dorian, *The English Diodatis* (New Brunswick: Rutgers University Press, 1950), pp. 168–73.

[35] *CPW*, I: 1624–1642, ed. by Don M. Wolfe (1953), pp. 809–10.

[36] *Minor Poems*, pp. 154–67. According to Arthur S. P. Woodhouse and Douglas Bush, even the two pastoral odes entitled *L'Allegro* and *Il Penseroso* have links with the genre of the academic encomium: see *A Variorum Commentary on the Poems of John Milton*, 2 vols (London: Routledge & Kegan Paul, 1970–72), II: *The Minor English Poems* (1972), pp. 227–28; see *Minor Poems*, pp. 34–47.

[37] *Minor Poems*, pp. 308–09 (ll. 126 and 135).

wrote a poem dedicated to Dati and entitled *Doversi andare peregrinando il mondo per acquistar fama*, which begins with the line 'Lungi dal Ciel natio mercar onori' and clearly draws on his own ode prefaced to Milton's *Poems*:

> Di bella gloria amante
> Milton dal Ciel natio per varie parti
> Le peregrine piante
> Volgesti a ricercar scienze, ed arti.[38]

Among the the many literary academies that flourished in Florence at that time, Dati and Francini were two young protagonists in the 'virtuosa conversazione' held in the house of the lawyer Agostino Coltellini (1613–1693), later called 'Università' and since 1637 formally known as 'Accademia degli Apatisti'[39] — the 'Dispassionates', or as in the cathartic conclusion of Milton's *Samson Agonistes* (1671): 'all passion spent'. The name was coined by Benedetto Fioretti (1579–1642) in his first two volumes of *Proginnasmi poetici*, published under the pseudonym of 'Udeno Nisieli da Vernio, Accademico Apatista'.[40] Lippi was one of its earliest members, and the first cantari of the *Malmantile* were regularly read in this academy since 1649.[41] The antiquarian Anton Francesco Gori recorded 'Giovanni Milton inglese' as a member in 1638.[42] Dati soon became secretary, and 'Censor perpetuo' was the eminent grammarian Benedetto Buonmattei, to whom Milton addressed his only extant letter from Florence.[43]

[38] See ibid., p. 160 (ll. 37–40). Cf. *Delle Poesie varie del Sigr. Gio. Antonio Francini dottore nell'una, e nell'altra legge, & Academico Apatista. Parte prima* (Paris: Brunet, 1644), pp. 15–19 (p. 15).
[39] See Edoardo Benvenuti, *Agostino Coltellini e l'Accademia degli Apatisti a Firenze nel secolo XVII* (Pistoia: Officina Tipografica Cooperativa, 1910), pp. 38–42, 233–81. *La Sfinge*'s enigmatic sonnet 'Con un picciol coltello il sen m'aprì' (p. 117, III. 11) is dedicated to Coltellini's circle; cf. BNCF, MS Magl. VII. 359, fol. 301[v].
[40] Benedetto Fioretti, *Proginnasmi poetici di Udeno Nisieli da Vernio, Accademico Apatista*, 5 vols (Florence: Pignoni, 1620–39).
[41] See *Il Seicento fiorentino: Arte a Firenze da Ferdinando I a Cosimo III*, ed. by Comitati Raffaello e Seicento fiorentino (Florence: Cantini, 1986), p. 343. On Lippi, 'ancor'egli Accademico Apatista', see Benvenuti, p. 254. In 1669 the Apatista Lorenzo Magalotti, who will be the first translator of Milton's *Paradise Lost*, donated a manuscript copy of *Il Mamantile* to the 'merrie monarch' Charles II: see Anna M. Crinò, 'Dono di L. Magalotti a Carlo II', in *Fatti e figure del Seicento anglo-toscano: documenti inediti sui rapporti letterari, diplomatici, culturali fra Toscana e Inghilterra* (Florence: Olschki, 1957), pp. 123–26.
[42] Anton F. Gori, *Discorso recitato nella celebre Accademia degli Apatisti* (1754), Biblioteca Marucelliana, Florence, MS A. 36, partly published in Alessandro Lazzeri, *Intellettuali e consenso nella Toscana del Seicento: l'Accademia degli Apatisti* (Milan: Giuffrè, 1983), pp. 57–121 (p. 74). See Estelle Haan, *From Academia to Amicitia: Milton's Latin Writings and the Italian Academies* (Philadelphia: American Philosophical Society, 1998), pp. 29–52.
[43] *Life Records*, I, 382–89; cf. Lazzeri, p. 67. See *Vita di Benedetto Buommattei scritta da Dalisto Narceate* [Giovanni Battista Casotti] *Pastore Arcade*, in Benedetto Buonmattei, *Della lingua Toscana: libri due* (Florence: Guiducci & Franchi, [1623–43] 1714), pp. 1–61 (pp. 31–33).

Notwithstanding the possibility that many learned societies were essentially created 'per andare a caccia alle lodi', as Dati ironically wrote in a *censura* of an academic sonnet,[44] Coltellini's academy stood out and was 'fra tutte le consorelle di Firenze e delle altre città una delle più utili e più di ogni altra feconda', as Michele Maylender wrote in his *Storia delle Accademie d'Italia*.[45] Dino Provenzal commented that 'pareva il tribunale supremo dello spirito'.[46] The Apatisti Academy, in addition, was particularly open to young scholars and foreign literati, as Coltellini had made its mission to be 'l'istituzione della gioventù nelle case civili' and 'il servigio de' forestieri massime oltramontani'.[47] According to the literary historian Salvino Salvini, for instance, Dati's house was 'la Magione de' Letterati, particolarmente Oltramontani',[48] and Milton's warm reception is a notable example.

One of the most active and extravagant members of the Apatisti was undoubtedly Malatesti, who joined the academy in 1635 together with Dati. Following the characteristic self-fashioning of the Apatisti, he adopted the anagrammatic name 'Aminta Setaiolo', with reference to his current profession as a silk merchant and to Tasso's seminal pastoral drama *Aminta* (1573).[49] As a sign of appreciation from his fellow academicians, the first edition of Malatesti's *Sfinge* included a proemial erudite letter on enigmatography by Dati, a dedicatory sonnet and a Latin epigram by Coltellini.

Milton's biographer David Masson suggests that it may have been precisely Malatesti who introduced the English poet to 'the blind sage',[50] namely to 'the famous Galileo grown old, a prisoner to the Inquisition', who championed

[44] See Gaetano Imbert, *La vita fiorentina nel Seicento, secondo memorie sincrone (1644–1670)* (Florence: Bemporad & Figlio, 1906), p. 169: 'Ingegni men che mediocri venivan levati alle stelle, tutti erano chiarissimi e illustri. Tutti, oimè tutti, passavano per poeti!'

[45] Michele Maylender, *Storia delle Accademie d'Italia*, 5 vols (Bologna: Cappelli, 1926–30), I (1926), 219–26 (p. 219).

[46] Dino Provenzal, *La Vita e le opere di Lodovico Adimari* (Rocca S. Casciano: Cappelli, 1902), p. 4.

[47] BR, MS 1949; cf. Benvenuti, pp. 255–56.

[48] Salvino Salvini, *Fasti Consolari dell'Accademia Fiorentina* (Florence: Tarini e Franchi, 1717), p. 548.

[49] Lazzeri, p. 69. See Corinna Salvadori, Peter Brand, and Richard Andrews, *Overture to the Opera: Italian Pastoral Drama in the Renaissance. Poliziano's 'Orfeo' and Tasso's 'Aminta' with Facing English Translations* (Dublin: UCD Foundation for Italian Studies, 2013), pp. 79–199. From Tasso's major epic poem, *Gerusalemme liberata* (1581), in 1633 the Apatisti Academy also took its motto: 'Oltre i confini ancor del mondo nostro' (XIV. 35. 8) (see *Fasti Consolari*, p. 609). Giovanni Prezziner explains that the motto was chosen 'forse per denotare che la sua fama sarebbesi estesa per ogni dove, o per indicare che tra' suoi Membri si sarebbero presto contati molti Dotti oltramonani': *Storia del pubblico studio e delle società scientifiche e letterarie di Firenze*, 2 vols (Florence: Carlo, 1810), I, 80.

[50] David Masson, *The Life of John Milton: Narrated in Connexion with the Political, Ecclesiastical, and Literary History of his Time*, 7 vols (London: Macmillan, 1859–94), I (1859), 737.

freedom of thought while the learned men of Italy 'did nothing but bemoan the servile condition into which learning amongst them was brought', as Milton recalled in his *Areopagitica* (1644).[51] Milton's actual visit to Galileo has been variously disputed, but Dati's last letter from Florence, dated December 1648, sends the greetings of a 'Galilei' among others, probably Galileo's son Vincenzo (1606–1649), who was also an Apatista.[52] However, the only passing mention of Malatesti's name in Milton's writings is in a letter to Dati of April 1647.[53] In a later autobiographical passage of the *Defensio secunda* (1654), in which the already completely blind Secretary for Foreign Tongues listed his unforgettable friends of the Florentine academies, we find Dati, Francini, and Coltellini, but not Malatesti.[54] Why, then, such ungenerous memory?

In many respects Malatesti was a 'problematic figure' among the academicians.[55] Initially, Milton's attitude could be related to a difference in personality and 'education'. Still around 1637, for example, Milton held that Italian language was a degenerate form of Latin,[56] and Malatesti — unlike Dati or Francini, who is acknowledged in the *Malmantile* as 'il più valente | perch'egli sapea leggere i Latini' (III. 28. 1–2) —, was not trained in classical languages. Nevertheless, he was so strongly motivated to acquire a reading knowledge of Latin that, in an elegant booklet in 32s dated 1630, he had began an Italian translation of the *Janua linguarum* (1611) by the Irish Jesuit William Bathe. This Latin textbook was quite innovative, and Timothy Corcoran observed that the Italian translation of this work 'was drawn into the last of the great wars in the history of post-Renaissance scholarship'.[57] Unfortunately, the young Malatesti never completed his translation, nor ever really learned to read Latin, as Magliabechi

---

[51] *CPW*, II: 1643–1648, ed. by Ernest Sirluck (New Haven: Yale University Press, 1959), pp. 537–38. The recent memory of Galileo imprisoned and blind might have contributed to the inspiration of *Samson Agonistes*, first published in 1671, but perhaps composed in the late 1640s, as heterodoxically (yet not unconvincingly) conjectured by William Riley Parker: see *Milton: A Biography*, 2 vols (Oxford: Clarendon Press, 1968), II, 903–17.

[52] *Life Records*, II: 1639–51 (1950), 222. At the time of Milton's visit, Galileo was perhaps at Vincenzo's house in Costa San Giorgio to 'receive medical treatment', not in Arcetri as usually reported: see Neil Harris, 'Galileo as Symbol: the "Tuscan artist" in *Paradise Lost*', *Annali dell'Istituto e Museo di Storia della Scienza di Firenze*, 10 (1985), 3–29 (p. 7). Cf. Marjorie Nicolson, 'Milton and the Telescope', *English Literary History*, 2 (1935), 1–32 (pp. 8–10).

[53] *Life Records*, II, 187. On the long correspondence between Milton and Dati, see Haan, pp. 53–60.

[54] *CPW*, IV: 1650–1655, ed. by Don M. Wolfe (1966), 616–17.

[55] See Anthony M. Cinquemani, *Glad to Go for a Feast: Milton, Buonmattei, and the Florentine Accademici* (New York: Lang, 1998), p. 27.

[56] See 'Ad Patrem', in *Minor Poems*, pp. 274–76 (l. 83). Cf. Ernest Sirluck, 'Milton's Idle Right Hand', *Journal of English and Germanic Philology*, 60 (1961), 749–85 (pp. 784–85); and Douglas Bush, 'The Date of Milton's *Ad Patrem*', *Modern Philology*, 61/63 (1963–64), 204–08.

[57] Timothy Corcoran, *Studies in the History of Classical Teaching: Irish and Continental, 1500–1700* (London: Longmans, Green and Co., 1911), p. 115. See *Janua Linguarum tradotta in volgare da Ant. Malatesti 1630* (BNCF, MS Magl. VII. 237, fols 1–29ʳ); cf. William Bathe,

clearly stated in a letter of November 1671 to the bibliographer Angelico Aprosio, explaining that Malatesti did not own Latin books because 'non intende la Lingua Latina', but 'dissimula tal cosa, e vuol mostrare d'intenderla'.[58]

It is not as an erudite scholar, in fact, but as a 'rustic poet' that Malatesti will be remembered in connection with Milton's visit to Florence. In 1637, in his villa in Taiano, Malatesti completed 'a cycle of fifty amusingly obscene sonnets in the baroque idiom', as Constantinos Patrides described them, later dedicated and presented to Milton: *La Tina, equivoci rusticali*.[59] Tina is the name of the rustic muse and mistress of a fictional peasant poet called Nencio, whose name only occurs in the dedicatory prose letter *Nencio alla Tina*.[60] In the tradition of love poetry, Malatesti's equivocations happily fail to live up to the name of the great ancestor Malatesta 'dei Sonetti', a contemporary of Francesco Petrarca. In the first sonnet, the author calls them 'sonetti con la coda', but this is not really an addition to the group of tailed sonnets later included in *La Sfinge*: the 'tail' of lines which would define this stylistic variant is always missing, since it is just the phallic metaphor of a *cauda salacis*.[61] It is to the genre of Florentine burlesque poetry that *La Tina* ultimately belongs.

Ianua linguarum, seu modus maxime accomodatus, quo patefit aditus ad omnes linguas intelligendas (Salamanca: Cea Tesa, 1611). The first Italian translation of this work had just been published in Milan in 1628 by the German scholar (and Catholic convert) Caspar Schoppe, under the pseudonym 'Pascasius Grosippus' (see Corcoran, pp. 115–30).

[58] In another letter to Aprosio of December 1672, immediately after the poet's death, Magliabechi wrote: 'È morto in compendio il Malatesti: i suoi libri si venderanno, ma però son tutti in lingua Toscana, già che la latina esso non la intendeva'. The two letters are quoted by Achille Neri in his notice on Malatesti published in *Il Propugnatore: studi filologici, storici e bibliografici di vari soci della Commissione pe' Testi di Lingua*, 6/1 (1873), 90–112 (pp. 98, 101).

[59] John Milton, *Selected Prose*, ed. by Constantinos A. Patrides (Columbia: University of Missouri Press, 1985), p. 20. It is perhaps because of the date of composition that French inserts the 'poetic tribute' in September 1638 (*Life Records*, I, 375–76); however, it is also possible that Malatesti prepared and presented the dedicated copy of his sonnets on the occasion of Milton's return to Florence in March 1639 (see ibid., pp. 407–14).

[60] In the 1650 MS the letter follows the sonnets (Magl. VII. 233, fols 50ʳ–56ʳ), but in the MS dedicated to Milton it is more suitably placed as a preface; the variant 'talento' instead of 'giudizio', in the sentence 's'io ti do tutto quel poco di [giudizio] ch'io mi trovo' (*Tina*, NLS, fol. 9ᵛ), confirms that the 1637 letter is the earliest version; for a comparison between the 1650 MS and the printed editions, see A. Malatesti, *La Tina*, ed. by Mirella Masieri (Rome: Salerno Editrice, 2005), pp. 99–112 (in part. pp. 103–05).

[61] De Miranda comments: '*La Tina* è un gioco greve che culmina in ogni poesia nelle sconcezze della strofa finale. La chiarezza espressiva delle liriche contrasta con la natura oscura dell'ispirazione, misogina e ossessiva. La donna è un oggetto da usare, trastullo o nemico, solo deuteragonista in una trama fatta di burle e pratiche sessuali che rivelano disprezzo e, forse, tendenze omosessuali. L'omaggio a Milton è concepibile solo nell'ambito di un *milieu* libertino, lì dove erano quasi d'obbligo una duplice personalità, l'abito conformista e uno spirito anticonformista' (p. 115). As Malatesti concluded his epistolary poem addressed to Lippi with 'cinquanta reverenze', it is also possible that the poet initially wanted to dedicate *La Tina* to Lippi (*Lettera familiare*, p. 15).

The dedicated manuscript of *La Tina* illustrates well the point made by the Veronese lawyer Giovanni Fratta in a 1590 dialogue: modern dedications, he wrote, are often 'd'incerto honore a chiunque si dedicano, per l'obliqua dispositione di molti Scrittori'.[62] The dedication is in the form of a stone-tablet inscription, which seems to commemorate Milton's passage in Florence *et in Arcadia*, thus appearing in ironic contrast to the pastoral elegies that the young English poet might have recited among the Apatisti. If 'Milton in Italy was an oxymoron in search of the higher resolutions of paradox', as he is well characterized by Susanne Woods,[63] Malatesti's gift was a kind of 'paradoxical encomium', somewhat like the *cicuta* mentioned among the other Tuscan gifts, which can be a shepherd's pipe or a deadly ironic Socratic poison. *La Tina* caricatures the 'association of rural labour with ignorance — in contrast with the idealizing tendency of classical pastoral', which 'seems to have been a habit for Milton', as Sarah Knight pointed out.[64] Besides, if there is any musicality in Malatesti's verses, he certainly did not make any effort 'to smooth and make them gentle from rustick harshness and distemper'd passions', as Milton put it in his treatise *On Education* (1644),[65] quite the contrary.

Milton probably shipped the manuscript to London in 1639, in the 'Parcel of curious and rare Books which he had pick'd up in his Travels', as related by his nephew Edward Phillips.[66] Masson further imagines that *La Tina* 'must have lain among his papers all his life — turned up now and then with a grim smile of recognition when he was looking for something else'.[67] But the signs of such recognition are even scarcer than the information about Milton's Florentine period.

---

[62] Giovanni Fratta, *Della Dedicatione de' Libri, con la Correttion dell'Abuso, in questa materia introdotto* (Venice: Angelieri, 1590), p. 1; see *Uso e abuso delle dediche: a proposito del 'Della dedicatione de' libri' di Giovanni Fratta*, ed. by Marco Santoro (Rome: Edizioni dell'Ateneo, 2006).

[63] Susanne Woods, '"That Freedom of Discussion Which I loved": Milton's Italian Journey and Cultural Self-definition', in *Milton in Italy: Contexts, Images, Contradictions*, ed. by Mario A. Di Cesare (Binghamton, NY: MRTS, 1991), pp. 9–18 (p. 9).

[64] Sarah Knight, 'Milton and the Idea of the University', in *Young Milton*, ed. by Jones, pp. 137–60 (p. 150).

[65] *CPW*, II, 357–415 (p. 411). Milton's treatise witnesses his commitment to the philosophical principles of the Czech educator John Amos Comenius, whose successful *Janua Linguarum Reserata* (1631) was strongly influenced by Bathe's work.

[66] Edward Phillips, *The Life of Mr. John Milton* (1694), in *The Early Lives of Milton*, ed. by Helen Darbishire (London: Constable, 1932), pp. 49–82 (p. 59).

[67] Masson, p. 735. Jackson Campbell Boswell classified the manuscript with the letter 'V', meaning that 'the work was in Milton's library or that there is sufficient internal evidence in his works to indicate that he read it', although he misspelled the title as 'La Trina', which could be read as either a 'lacework' or the Italian word for 'lavatory': see *Milton's Library: A Catalogue of the Remains of John Milton's Library and an Annotated Reconstruction of Milton's Library and Ancillary Readings* (New York: Garland, 1975), p. 163.

It is plausible that Malatesti's gift was primarily meant as an 'academic prank' to test Milton's linguistic skills and tease his morality.[68] To be sure, the prank went well 'beyond the Puritanic pale', as Edward K. Rand suggested about Milton's period of academic 'rustication' at Cambridge.[69] Considering the self-image that the English poet was carefully pursuing through his Italian journey, and given his concern with the 'novae cicutae',[70] it is understandable that he would have wanted to overlook Malatesti's gift. Sten Bodvar Liljegren sharply infers Milton's over-serious contempt 'from the fact that he does not include the name of Malatesti when he proudly enumerates his other Florence "celebrities", though Malatesti undoubtedly appears as the one who was the most prominent of them all'.[71] It could well be argued that the association with the author of such indecent equivocations might have undermined Milton's rhetorical self-defence, or even simply his advocacy for the institution of similar academies in England. However, these arguments appear overall weak.

To begin with, Milton had already a reputation at Cambridge for the licentious jokes that then enlivened academic orations on special occasions; it suffices to mention his sixth Prolusion, which is not only full of 'salt' and has some coarse puns on the 'sphinx', but where he also suggests that his nickname, 'the Lady' (*Domina*), may have originated from the fact that his 'hand has never grown horny with driving the plough'.[72] As Edward Le Comte has shown, there is much evidence of a 'sly' and 'ambiguous' Milton,[73] who may have relished Malatesti's equivocations. In the preface to his English translation of *La Tina*, Donald Sears precisely argued that Milton's punning invectives against the 'Gallus Morus', namely the Franco-Scottish preacher Alexander More, provide 'the strongest indication that Milton was recalling Malatesti'.[74] Moreover, in the *Defensio*

---

[68] See Anna K. Nardo, 'Milton and the Academic Sonnet', in *Milton in Italy*, ed. by Di Cesare, pp. 489–503 (p. 499). Mario Praz suggests that Malatesti could be seen as a character featured in the painting *Le burle di Pievano Arlotto* by Baldassarre Franceschini, and considers that he presented to Milton his 'libretto di versi grassocci [...] per farsi gioco della sua severa castità' (*Storia della letteratura inglese* (Florence: Sansoni, 1937), p. 158). But Giuseppe Tomasi di Lampedusa contends that Milton 'non si offese neppure per i detestabili e volgari versi che un letteratucolo, il Malatesti, gli dedicò per schernire la severità dei suoi costumi': see *Opere*, ed. by Gioacchino Lanza Tomasi and Nicoletta Polo (Milan: Mondadori, 2006), pp. 845–46.

[69] Edward K. Rand, 'Milton in rustication', *Studies in Philology*, 19 (1922), 109–35 (p. 132).

[70] *Minor Poems*, pp. 310–11. Cf. Albert C. Labriola, 'Portraits of an Artist: Milton's Changing Self-Image', *Milton Studies*, 19 (1984), 179–94 (p. 185).

[71] Liljegren further comments: 'Such a gift must be regarded either as complimentary in front of another lascivious mind, or as a sneer at somebody whom the author regards as a silly bore' ('Milton at Florence', *Neophilologus*, 43 (1959), 133–37 (p. 136).

[72] See *CPW*, I, 266–306 (pp. 278 and 283–84); on the nickname, see *John Milton: Life, Work, and Thought*, ed. by Gordon Campbell and Thomas N. Corns (Oxford: Oxford University Press, 2008), p. 60.

[73] See Edward Le Comte, *Milton Re-viewed: Ten Essays* (New York: Garland, 1991).

[74] '*La Tina*: The Country Sonnets of Malatesti as Dedicated to Mr. John Milton, English

secunda Coltellini is mentioned despite the fact that in 1652, when Malatesti was appointed 'Apatista reggente',[75] under the academic anagram 'Ostilio Contalgeni' Coltellini had just published his *Rime piacevoli*, a collection of not always subtle and often obscene double-entendres written 'in campagna'.[76] On the other hand, Malatesti was mainly known and appreciated for his riddles, while the equivocal sonnets dedicated to Milton were practically unknown outside Florence, let alone to English readers.

We could put forward another hypothesis to tentatively account for Milton's caution as regards Malatesti's *equivoci*. As explained by Mario Praz, 'equivocation' was a characteristic figure of speech of the Jesuits, 'a perfect counterpart of Machiavellian dissimulation', and it 'became a byword in England since Henry Garnet, superior of the Jesuits in England, used it during his trial for complicity in the Gunpowder Plot'.[77] To the 'proditio bombardica' the young Milton had dedicated the minor epic poem *In Quintum Novembris* (1626), in which Satan is a Machiavellian advisor of the Pope and recommends the use of any trickery and fraud against the heretics.[78] In *Paradise Lost* (1667–74), Galileo's telescope is not different from Satan's cannon, loaded with 'spiritous' gunpowder.[79] It may be noted here that in the dedicatory prose letter of *La Tina* the ardent fictional poet warns that the devil might bring him to put 'fuoco alla bombarda': in the Tuscan literary idiom the phrase simply means 'to engage in polemics' and, in the erotic vocabulary, 'to engage in sodomy' — but it is possible that such double-entendres might have resonated with more *risqué* overtones in the different political and historical context, all the more so with a less Italianate reader than Milton.

More relevantly, perhaps, in the *Defensio Secunda* Milton claims that during his stay in Rome he was warned to return to Florence for his own safety, because

---

Gentleman', trans. by Donald Sears, *Milton Studies*, 13 (1979), 275–317 (p. 280). See *CPW*, IV, 564–71; cf. *Pro Se Defensio* (1655), where More is portrayed as a boar with 'tusk' and 'tail', ibid., pp. 698–825 (p. 746). Allodoli suggested that More's friendship with the Florentine literati may have been the reason why the correspondence with Dati ended relatively soon, in 1648, if not the reason why Milton's presence in Florence was hardly recorded by his friends: see Ettore Allodoli, *Giovanni Milton e l'Italia* (Prato: Vestri & Spighi, 1907), pp. 16–17. For intertextual parallels between *La Tina* and Milton's invective against More, see Allan H. Gilbert, 'Milton's Defense of Bawdry', *SAMLA Studies in Milton*, ed. by J. Max Patrick (Gainesville: University of Florida Press, 1953), pp. 54–71 (pp. 59–60).

[75] Lazzeri, p. 107.

[76] *Rime piacevoli d'Ostilio Contalgeni Accademico Apatista* (Florence: Massi, 1652), p. 8; the dedication of *Le lodi del salsicciotto*, dated May 1637, well exemplifies the bawdy character of these rustic verses (p. 68).

[77] Mario Praz, *Machiavelli and the Elizabethans: Annnual Italian Lecture of the British Academy* (London: Milford, 1928), p. 39.

[78] *Minor Poems*, pp. 236–54 (p. 244); see Wyman Herendeen, 'Milton and Machiavelli: The Historical Revolution and Protestant Poetics', in *Milton in Italy*, ed. by Di Cesare, pp. 427–44.

[79] John Milton, *Paradise Lost*, ed. by Alastair Fowler, rev. 2nd edn (Harlow: Longman, 2007), p. 362 (VI. 479).

some 'English Jesuits' were organizing 'plots' (*insidiae*) against him.[80] There is no evidence for this claim, but we can certainly read the poet's self-representation as an enemy of the Jesuits in connection with his new polemical position against the Presbyterians. At the beginning of *The Tenure of Kings and Magistrates* (1649), Milton compared 'these men' to the witches of *Macbeth* (1606), who 'palter with us in a double sense' (v. 9. 20).[81] The subtextual reference associates the Presbyterians with the Jesuits, summoned by Shakespeare's allusion to Garnet as the 'equivocator'. We could well imagine, then, that Milton 'turned up' Malatesti's manuscript when he composed his twenty-line sonnet *On the New Forcers of Conscience Under the Long Parliament* (c. 1647), probably the first tailed sonnet in English and a singular piece in his collection, which again identifies the Presbyterian's 'plots and packing' with 'those of *Trent*', with an etymological pun: '*New Presbyter* is but *Old Priest* writ Large'.[82] Precisely on account of his strong humour and liking for jokes, Christopher Hill called Milton 'the great equivocator', and argued that 'equivocation is at the heart of his greatest poetry'.[83]

While the reason for his silence on Malatesti remains conjectural, it is significant that the manuscript of *La Tina* seems to have vanished upon Milton's death. After a serendipitous find in the middle of the eighteenth century, at a book stall in London, it was copied and used for the *princeps* edition. Then it disappeared again, and its location remained unknown for the last two hundred years. In a 1959 paper, Samuel Kliger speculated that the manuscript may have been donated to Harvard University and destroyed in the library's great fire of 1764.[84]

---

[80] *CPW*, IV, 619. This circumstance would make a case against the fact that Milton could have met Galileo on his second visit to Florence.

[81] See *CPW*, III: 1648–1649, ed. by Merritt Y. Hughes (1962), p. 191: the Presbyterians 'have juggl'd and palter'd with the world, bandied and born armes against thir King, devested him, disannointed him, nay curs'd him all over in thir Pulpits and thir Pamphlets'. Nicholas Mcdowell explains: 'There seems to be an echo in the repeated *d*s of the passage from the *Tenure* quoted above ("divested him, disanointed him") of the famous charge made by Edward Coke against Garnet at his trial that he was "a Doctor of Dissimulation, Deposing of Princes, Disposing of Kingdoms, Daunting and Deterring of subjects, and Destruction"' ('Milton's Regicide Tracts and the Uses of Shakespeare', in *The Oxford Handbook of Milton*, ed. by Nicholas McDowell and Nigel Smith (Oxford: Oxford University Press, 2009), pp. 252–71 (p. 261).

[82] *Minor Poems*, p. 71. Cf. the 'critical note' by Egerton Webbe to his *Sonnet to a Fog* (*Bentley's Miscellany*, ed. by Charles Dickens, William Harrison Ainsworth, and Albert Smith (London: Bentley, 1837), pp. 371–72), which concludes the explanation of the satyric effect of the 'coda' with the discussion of Milton's example and the words 'ex tempore' — we could see in this respect the *Extempore upon a Faggot* maliciously attributed to Milton in Elijah Fenton's *Oxford and Cambridge Miscellany Poems* (London: Lintott, 1708), p. 286.

[83] Christopher Hill, *Milton and the English Revolution* (London: Faber and Faber, 1977; repr. 1997), p. 472.

[84] Samuel Kliger, 'Milton in Italy and the Lost Malatesti Manuscript,' *Studies in Philology*, 51 (1954), 208–13 (p. 213).

The mystery of the original manuscript only added interest to the 'academic prank' in which Milton was involved, and *La Tina* was reprinted several times. The many editions, though, remained fundamentally destitute of critical value: without the original, as Ettore Allodoli concluded in his 1913 edition, the attribution of this work to Malatesti was 'soltanto ipotetica, sebbene fondata su verisimiglianze sensatissime';[85] and in 1945 Sebastiano Blancato further suggested that 'anche la dedica al Milton rimane puramente ipotetica'.[86] A critical edition of *La Tina* was published by Clemente Valacca in 1914, together with a collection of forty madrigals entitled *La Geva*, by Alessandro Allegri (1560–1629).[87] This edition was based on the only holograph of the sonnets which was then available at the National Library of Florence, namely *La Tina da Castello*, but the manuscript is dated 1650 and dedicated to the Florentine gentleman Francesco Cordini, two sonnets are missing, four are replaced, there are significant variants, and the overall order seems less convincing.[88]

The 1637 manuscript dedicated to Milton, however, did exist: it had been kept since the 1820s at the Advocates Library in Edinburgh, where Walter Scott had served twice as a curator, and subsequently preserved in the National Library of Scotland.[89] Malatesti's 'rustic equivocations' arrived in Edinburgh at a time of great ferment for the Scottish literary culture, during the transformation of rural modernity at the 'Borders of Romanticism',[90] as differently expressed by the 'Heaven-taught ploughman' Robert Burns and the 'Ettrick Shepherd' James

---

[85] *La Sfinge*, p. ix. After all, *La Tina* is not even mentioned by Giulio Negri among the other works of 'Antonio Malatesta': see *Istoria degli scrittori fiorentini* (Ferrara: Pomatelli, 1722), pp. 63–64.

[86] Antonio Malatesti, *La Tina*, ed. by S. Blancato (Milan: Il Ruscello, 1945), p. 20.

[87] See Clemente Valacca, 'Prefazione', in A. Malatesti, *La Tina da Castello: aggiuntavi La Geva di Alessandro Allegri* (Messina: Principato, 1914), pp. 1–7.

[88] *La Tina da Castello: equivoci rusticali di Antonio Malatesti dedicati al Sig.ᵉ Franc.º Cordini. Con altre Poesie del Medes.ᵐᵒ, 1650*, BNCF, MS Magl. VII. 233; see also the anonymous copy in Magl. VII. 349; and Biscioni, fol. 271ᵛ, p. 1278. The same manuscript was used by Masieri in her 2005 critical edition of *La Tina*. Cordini actively participated in the private *conversazione* of the 'Percossi' organized by the painter Salvator Rosa, 'un teatrino di commedia improvvisa, ove tutti, anche le donne, erano… uomini', which included Malatesti, Lippi, Dati, Chimentelli, Torricelli, and many other members of the Florentine elite (Alterocca, p. 14).

[89] NLS, Adv. MS 19. 3. 40; see *Summary Catalogue of the Advocates' Manuscripts* (Edinburgh: HMSO, 1971), p. 87. With the exception of legal books, the library of the Faculty of Advocates was gifted to the NLS upon its establishment in 1925: see *For the Encouragement of Learning: Scotland's National Library 1689–1989*, ed. by Patrick Cadell and Ann Matheson (Edinburgh: HMSO, 1989). Sir Walter had been a curator in 1795–99 and 1805–09.

[90] See *Scotland and the Borders of Romanticism*, ed. by Leith Davis, Ian Duncan, and Janet Sorensen (Cambridge: Cambridge University Press, 2004); cf. I. Duncan, 'Edinburgh, Capital of the Nineteenth Century', in *Romantic Metropolis: Cultural Productions of the City, 1770–1840*, ed. by James Chandler and Kevin Gilmartin (Cambridge: Cambridge University Press, 2005), pp. 45–64.

Hogg. The following section outlines the history of the manuscript, once again 'recovered for the curious' among Milton's scholars,[91] and 'racquistato' for the students of Tuscan poetry.

3. 'La Tina' Regained: Manuscript, Copies, Print

The original manuscript of La Tina consisted of thirty-two leaves of fine laid paper,[92] later bound in green morocco together with handwritten leaves of Notizie intorno all'Autore and notes by Thomas Hollis of Lincoln's Inn (1720–1774) — 'the strenuous Whig, who used to send over Europe presents of democratical books'.[93] In the first note, dated 8 September 1758, Hollis reports that the manuscript was 'found at a stall in London 1757 by Thomas Brand Esquire of the Hide in Essex'.[94] The dedication of the Florentine manuscript must have sparked Brand's curiosity,[95] and he purchased it as a present for his dear friend and later benefactor Hollis, who had a keen interest in Milton and had travelled repeatedly to Florence in search of the young poet's memorabilia.

The Notizie on Malatesti are in the handwriting of the literary critic Giuseppe Baretti, a friend and protégé of Dr Johnson, but Hollis's second note informs that the text was 'chiefly taken from a Letter of D.ʳ Gio. Lami of Florence, written to D.ʳ Giovanni Marsili of Venice, now in London'.[96] In a letter from London to the Florentine historian Giovanni Lami,[97] dated 16 June 1758, the Venetian botanist

---

[91] Masson, p. 735.

[92] The original leaves are watermarked with a Latin cross in a pointed oval above illegible initials. This watermark was common among seventeenth-century papermakers, but it was particularly used in Genoese papers made for Spain and Portugal: see Edward Heawood, Watermarks, Mainly of the 17th and 18th Centuries (Hilversum: Paper Publications Society, 1950), p. 24, pls 144–45.

[93] James Boswell, Life of Johnson (1791), ed. by George B.N. Hill and Lawrence F. Powell, 6 vols (Oxford: Clarendon Press, 1934–50), IV, 97. See William H. Bond, Thomas Hollis of Lincoln's Inn: A Whig and his Books (Cambridge: Cambridge University Press, 1990). Cf. Allen Reddick, Thomas Hollis's Republican Books and the European Network: Anonymous Gifts on the Continent, 1750–1774 (Cambridge, MA: Harvard University Press, forthcoming).

[94] Tina, NLS, fol. 1ʳ. Cf. John Disney, Memoirs of Thomas Brand-Hollis, Esq. (London: Gillet, 1808), pp. 3 and 27, n. B.

[95] Under the dedication, on the same fol. 8ʳ, there are some handwritten marks which could be tentatively read as follows: the English date 'ye 2ⁿᵈ Nov 1684', the initials 'J.A.', and the signature 'TDeane'. The initials could be associated with the antiquary and mathematician John Aubrey, who drafted the Minutes of the Life of Mr. John Milton around 1681 (see Darbishire, pp. 1–15) and in 1682 acquired Milton's Defensio Secunda (see Anthony Powell, John Aubrey and his Friends, rev. edn (London: Hogarth, 1988), p. 298), but the handwriting does not seem to be his own.

[96] Tina, NLS, fol. 1ʳ. The Notizie are at fols 3ᵛ–7ᵛ.

[97] See Maria P. Paoli, 'Lami, Giovanni', DBI, 63 (2004), 226–33 (p. 227); cf. Maylender, I, 225. In 1748 Lami was also elected 'Apatista Reggente': see Novelle letterarie pubblicate a Firenze

and poet Giovanni Marsili asked for 'alcune notizie' on Malatesti and the rustic 'operetta' then owned by Hollis, 'curioso raccoglitore di tutto ciò che concerne o illustra la memoria del suo favorito Autore il gran Milton'; he also recommended the erudite librarian to send his reply directly to Hollis, whom he may have already met in Florence.[98] Lami promptly replied with a letter dated 15 July, as acknowledged by Hollis's note, but the current location of this letter (if extant) is unknown.

On 4 September, Marsili sent another letter to Lami, thanking him for the biographical note and announcing that on Friday 8 September he would be leaving London with 'un gran numero di libri nuovi e vecchi rari e curiosi', among which there was a copy of the *Equivoci rusticali* that Hollis wanted to be delivered to Lami in Florence as a sign of his gratitude.[99] In fact, the first of Hollis's two final notes, written in the folios added after the sonnets, records that on 8 September Hollis presented Marsili with a copy of *La Tina*, including the *Notizie* 'fairly written by Signor Baretti, & handsomely bound in vellum'.[100]

---

l'anno MDCCXLVIII (Florence: Stamperia della SS. Annunziata, 1748), coll. 389–90. See also Eric Cochrane, 'Florence in the 1740s: How Giovanni Lami Discovered the Past and Tried to Alter the Future', in *Florence in the Forgotten Centuries, 1527–1800* (Chicago and London: University of Chicago Press, 1973), pp. 317–96.

[98] *Lettere originali di Giovanni Lami*, BR, MS 3740, vol. 42, pp. 112–13. This letter was already transcribed (with minor errata) by Kliger, p. 212. Hollis probably met Marsili during his stay in Venice, between December 1750 and February 1751. Marsili was in London between 1757 and September 1758, when he became a member of the Royal Society. See Luigino Curti and Fernanda Menegalle, 'Giovanni Marsili', in *Professori e scienziati a Padova nel Settecento*, ed. by Sandra Casellato and Luciana Sitran Rea (Treviso: Antilia, 2002), pp. 304–12; and Luigi Melchiori, *Lettere e letterati a Venezia e a Padova a mezzo il secolo XVIII, da un carteggio inedito* (Padova: CEDAM, 1942), pp. 32–33, 58, 143–45.

[99] BR, MS 3740, vol. 42, p. 114. This letter was only partially transcribed by Kliger: 'La gentilissima lettera di V.S. Illma mi fu resa quasi negli estremi momenti della mia dimora in questo regno. Però non potrò soddisfare al desiderio suo d'essere da me informata delle nuove letterarie di queste parti, né al desiderio mio di servirla in tutto quello ch'io mai potessi. Porto meco un gran numero di libri nuovi e vecchi rari e curiosi, de' quali potrò far copia a V.S. Illma quando e quanto le piacerà, e a bocca le darò qualche ragguaglio della condizione presente delle lettere e delle arti in Inghilterra. Venerdì prossimo è il giorno fissato per la mia partenza. Farò un breve soggiorno in Olanda, e non mi tratterrò in Francia, se non quanto basti per abbracciare i miei amici. Quindi volerò alla mia bella et unica Italia, pigliando la via della Toscana per riveder la mia cara Firenze, e alcuni degli amici che mi sono rimasti costì, tra quali novero V.S. Illma come de' primi. Frattanto le rendo distinte grazie' etc (see Klieger, p. 212). Among Marsili's books, as explained by Marino Parenti, there may have been 'opere che, sotto l'etichetta della novellistica e del testo di lingua, nascondevano quella letteratura erotica che si definisce, pudicamente, con l'attributo "curiosa"': *Dizionario dei luoghi di stampa falsi, inventati o supposti* (Florence: Sansoni, 1951), p. 7.

[100] *Tina*, NLS, fol. 39^r/bis. Baretti and Marsili fell quickly apart after the latter's departure from London, as we can read in the second of the only two letters to Hollis left by Baretti, sent from Venice and dated 22 June 1763: see Giuseppe Baretti, *Lettere Sparse. Supplemento all'Epistolario*, ed. by Franco Fido (Turin: Centro Studi Piemontesi, 1976), p. 38. More revealing

The fourth and last note on the original manuscript, dated 26 September, informs us that Hollis sent another copy to the Accademia della Crusca, the oldest language academy in Europe, 'together with Milton's works 5 vol. quarto elegantly bound, & Toland's life of Milton'.[101] In a memorandum of the same day, as reported by Francis Blackburne, Hollis noted that the copy of *La Tina*, elegantly bound in vellum probably by Richard Montagu, was sent together with Milton's works to James Howe, a merchant of Livorno, 'to be forwarded free of charge whatsoever to Dr. John Marsili of Florence, to be presented by him (in full assembly) to the Academy of La Crusca'.[102] When Howe died, in 1760, the books passed to another English merchant based in Livorno, Francis Jermy, but were not presented to La Crusca until 1762, 'owing to the shameful behaviour of D.ʳ Marsili', as we read in Hollis' diary, on 8 May of that year.[103] The receipt was

---

is the caustic humour of the fictional letter sent to Marsili from London by the fine artist and Hollis's friend Giambattista Cipriani, in which Baretti attacked Marsili with crude metaphors taken from the tradition of rustic poetry, mocking his imminent probable appointment to the University of Padua — 'ogni elettore, satisfatto del tuo botanico sapere, non vorrà negarti la su' fava' — and asking some of his satirical poems, with the following note: 'Facilmente e con poca spesa troverai chi te le trascriva', perhaps with reference to his unacknowledged copies of *La Tina*: see Giuseppe Baretti, *La scelta delle lettere familiari*, ed. by Luigi Piccioni (Bari: Laterza, 1912), p. 141–42.

[101] Ibid. 'Before the Manuscript was written, ALL'ACCADEMIA DELLA CRUSCA | È DEDICATA QUESTA OPERETTA | TRATTA DA UN MANOSCRITTO ORIGINALE | TROVATO IN LONDRA L'ANNO MDCCLVIII'. The finding of the manuscript is deferred from 1757 to 1758, perhaps because of the Old Style calendar. On the Accademia della Crusca, 'probably the most famous of all Italian academies', see Frances A. Yates, 'The Italian Academies', in *Collected Essays*, 3 vols (London: Routledge, 1982–84), II: *Renaissance and Reform: The Italian Contribution* (1983), 6–29 (p. 20).

[102] Francis Blackburne, *Memoirs of Thomas Hollis* (London: Nichols, 1780), p. 491. It is possible that this 'John Marsili of Florence' was a homonym of the Venetian botanist, namely Giovanni, son of Alessandro Marsili from Siena, recorded as a member of the Apatisti in the year 1664 (Lazzeri, p. 95).

[103] Thomas Hollis, *Diary* (14 April, 1759–3 July, 1770), Houghton Library, Harvard University, Cambridge, MA, MS Eng 1191, transcr. by William H. Bond (Cambridge, MA: 1996), p. 115. Cf. Blackburne, p. 167. Unfortunately, it seems that we only have Hollis's diary from 1759 to 1770: see Arthur Ponsonby, *More English Diaries: Further Reviews of Diaries from the Sixteenth to the Nineteenth Century with an Introduction on Diary Reading* (London: Methuen & Co, 1927), pp. 101–09. The letter from La Crusca must have reignited Hollis's curiosity about Milton's visits to Florence. According to Blackburne, indeed, on 'May 14, 1762, Mr Hollis sent to examine the Laurentian library at Florence for some Italian poetry; and especially six sonnets of Milton addressed to his friend Chimentelli; and also some Italian and Latin compositions, and various original letters of Milton, said to be scattered in Florence. The inquirer was likewise commissioned to search for an original bust of Milton in marble', but nothing could be found (p. 167). In a footnote to his edition of Milton's poems, Thomas Warton ostensibly repeated this information but wrote that Hollis himself 'examined the Laurentian library at Florence': see J. Milton, *Poems Upon Several Occasions*, ed. by Thomas Warton (London: Dodsley, 1785) p. 338. From Hollis' *Diary* we only know that on 14 May, 1762, he spent 'most part of the morning writing for the foreign post' (p. 116).

acknowledged with a letter of thanks dated 18 March, sent by Rosso Antonio Martini, vice-secretary of the Academy, and the books were delivered by the lawyer Giovanni Paolo Ombrosi.[104]

Among the 'code magliabechiane' of the National Library of Florence there is a copy which seems in Hollis's original binding, and bears on the marbled inside cover the label 'Dell'Accademia della Crusca 1783'.[105] The dedication to La Crusca, placed on the verso of the folio which reproduces the dedication to Milton, is dated 1757; underneath, in different handwriting, is noted: 'di mano del Marchese Andrea Alamanni'. However, the Marquis Alamanni, vice-secretary of La Crusca since 1737, was found dead in his bed in 1753, having either committed suicide or been killed because of an acrimonious legal dispute, as suggested by Marquis Bernardo Tanucci:[106] in either case, there must be another explanation, as it is impossible that he could be the author of the copy of a manuscript found in 1757. It seems in fact to be Baretti's fair handwriting, not Alamanni's, and the watermark is the same as in some of the additional folios bound with the Edinburgh manuscript.[107]

In the rich collection of stolen books and manuscripts put together by Count Guglielmo Libri, then largely sold to Lord Bertram IV Ashburnham and finally

---

[104] See Blackburne, p. 738. The diary of the Academy written by Leonardo del Riccio, in March 1762, confirms: 'Finalm.te [il Segretario] presentò all'Accad.a l'opere sì di verso come di prosa del celebre Inglese Milton in cinque volumi; la vita dello stesso Milton scritta in idioma Inglese scritta dal Toland, e una raccolta di n.o 50 son.ti di Ant.o Malatesti intitol.ti = La Tina = e dallo Stesso dedicati al med.mo Milton e copiati diligentem.e a mano dall'autografo dell'Autore ora esist.e presso il Gentil.o Inglese che ha fatto questo generoso dono all'Accad.a Questi libri oltre l'opere stampati splendidam.e ed arricchiti di bellis.mi rami sono legati con lusso e con una magnific.za sorprend.te, e sono stati mandati dal Sig.re Francis Jermy ricco negoz.te Inglese di Liv.o unitam.te con una breve Lett.ra scritta in Inglese dal Donatore, che non ha voluto palesare il suo nome. Fu commesso al Segr.o di ringraziare per Lett.ra il Sig.re Jermy il quale di più avea trasmesso all'Accad.a li sud.i libri franchi di spesa' (Archivio Storico dell'Accademia della Crusca, Fascetta 78, MS 4394, p. 152). In the London section of Novelle letterarie, Lami also reported the donation, although La Tina is defined as 'Commedia in versi' (Florence: Albizzini, 9 April, 1762, n. 15, col. 250); cf. Kliger, p. 211.

[105] BNCF, MS Magl. VII. 1356; the binding in white vellum with gilt flourishes and the Britannia symbol on the cover is probably by Montagu: see Bond, pp. 42–49. Maura Scarlino Rolih includes this MS in the list of 'codici "fantasmi"', i.e. the Magliabechi MSS that 'non compaiono in nessuna delle descrizioni del fondo, né sull'inventario, né sul catalogo alfabetico, ma sono elencati per segnatura, in coda alle varie classi, sulla vacchetta, cioè sul repertorio numerico del fondo stesso, che certamente ha la sola utilità di garantire al bibliotecario che i pezzi ci sono materialmente' ('Code magliabechiane': un gruppo di manoscritti della Biblioteca Nazionale Centrale di Firenze fuori inventario, ed. by Maura Scarlino Rolih (Florence: La Nuova Italia, 1985) pp. v and 20). Some of these 'code' were listed by Paul O. Kristeller in his Iter Italicum (London: Warburg Institute, 1963–97), but many remain as yet uncharted.

[106] See Enrica Viviani Della Robbia, Bernardo Tanucci ed il suo più importante carteggio, 2 vols (Florence: Sansoni, 1942), II, 386–87.

[107] See below, Note on the Text; cf. Heawood, pll. 349–51.

purchased by the Biblioteca Laurenziana in Florence, there is an additional fair copy of Alamanni's copy of *La Tina*, made by the Arcadian priest Luigi Fiacchi (1754–1825), also author of *Sonetti pastorali* (1789). In his note to the text, Fiacchi explained that he decided not to include the 'notizie sulla vita dell'autore' present in Alamanni's copy because they were 'quasi le stesse che si trovano nella prefazione ai Sonetti Polifemici del Sud.° Poeta stampati da Bianchini e Salvini'.[108]

The 'sonetti polifemici' are Malatesti's *Brindisi de' Ciclopi*, published in 1673 with a brief address to the reader by the humanist doctor Giovanni Cinelli Calvoli (1625–1706), who had also first edited *Il Malmantile*.[109] The second edition of the *Brindisi* was published in 1723 by Giuseppe Manni, together with other sonnets of the same genre by Pietro Salvetti, 'Priore' of the Apatisti.[110] This second edition is particularly important, because it was enriched with annotations by the two erudite priests Giuseppe Maria Bianchini, who was also an active member of the Apatisti, and Anton Maria Biscioni, librarian of the Biblioteca Laurenziana, and included a long 'Prefazione' on dithyrambic poetry with substantial biographical notes on the two authors.[111] Pietro Fanfani largely drew from this preface for the first modern edition of *La Tina*, published in 1865.[112]

The main source of biographical information for Manni's preface was the entry on Malatesti in the manuscript *Selve per li Commentarj dell'Accademia degli Apatisti* drafted by the friar Francesco Cionacci (1633–1714), provided for the editors of the *Brindisi* by the Florentine Canon Salvino Salvini.[113] The preface is unsigned, and Salvini states that it is Bianchini 'che nella prefazione ci dà piena contezza del Malatesti';[114] however, it seems more likely that the preface was

---

[108] BML, MS Ashburnham-Libri 746. Following the unlikely attribution, Fiacchi noted: 'Il libro da cui fu tratta questa copia è scritto da And. Alamanni, e dicesi preso da un MS. originale trovato in Londra nel 1757. Esso libro apparteneva alla già Accademia della Crusca, ed ora trovasi nella Magliabechiana'. Cf. *Catalogue of the manuscripts at Ashburnham Place. Part the first comprising a collection formed by professor Libri* (London: Hodgson, 1853), n. 746: 'Manuscrit sur papier, in quarto, du XVIII [*sic*] siècle'.

[109] For Cinelli Calvoli's address, see *Brindis*, pp. 5–6.

[110] See Mario Aglietti, 'Avvertenza', in Pietro Salvetti, *Rime giocose edite e inedite di un umorista florentino del secolo XVII* (Florence: Bertelli, 1904), pp. 1–49 (p. 21).

[111] *Brindisi d'Antonio Malatesti e di Pietro Salvetti: con annotazioni. Dedicati all'Illustriss. Sig. Bindo Simone Peruzzi* (Florence: Manni, 1723). Bindo S. Peruzzi acted as vice-secretary of the Apatisti in 1720 (see Lazzeri, p. 121).

[112] Pietro Fanfani, 'Della poesia giocosa e di Antonio Malatesti', in A. Malatesti, *La Sfinge, I Brindisi de' Ciclopi e La Tina*, ed. by P. Fanfani (Milan: Corradetti e C., 1865), pp. v–xxxi; according to Fanfani, in 1637 Malatesti's sonnets were 'mandati poscia al suo amico Giovanni Milton in Inghilterra, tra le carte del quale debbono estere stati trovati in processo di tempo e dati alla stampa, fattane poi una seconda edizione pochi anni addietro in Firenze con la data di Londra' (p. xxx).

[113] *Brindisi*, ed. by Manni, pp. 23–24. Cionacci was, 'dopo la morte del Coltellini, il vero sostenitore e restauratore degli Apatisti' (Maylender, I, 224). He left two biographical sketches of Malatesti's life, but the second one seems a fair copy of the first with minor variants, entitled *Notizie del Sig. Antonio Malatesti* (MS Magl. IX. 50 no. 34, fols 134^{r-v} and 143^r).

drafted by Domenico Maria Manni (1690–1788), son of the publisher and author of other similar works.[114]

What is essential to note in our context is that the 1723 *Notizia* on Malatesti is, ostensibly, an extended version of the *Notizie* copied by Baretti (included in the present edition); therefore, Lami's 1758 letter was probably derived from this same earlier text. It is possible that Hollis had access to Manni's edition, which is the only one containing the quotation from the beginning of Petrarch's *Triumphus Famæ*: 'Che trae l'uom dal sepolcro, e 'n vita il serba' (I. 9), which Hollis copied in the first of the folios bound together with *La Tina* and used as his 'favourite "Liberty" quotation' in later presentation books.[116] If so, we can conjecture that it was Baretti who brought the book to Hollis's attention — and there is evidence, in fact, that Baretti checked or simply abridged the original version of Manni's preface. All the same, we can more simply assume that Hollis derived his Petrarchan quote from Chimentelli's ode prefaced to *La Sfinge*.

The copy of *La Tina* that Hollis presented to Marsili on 8 September is, unfortunately, still missing.[117] However, we know that it was used for the *princeps* edition, in ottavo, allegedly published in London by Thomas Edlin in 1757.[118] In the eighteenth century, many books of burlesque and erotic content were published with the fictitious imprint of 'London'. For instance, the important edition of *Sonetti del Burchiello, del Bellincioni e d'altri poeti fiorentini alla burchiellesca*, dated London 1757, was printed in Lucca and Pisa, and probably edited by Biscioni. Among other Italian works, in 1725 Edlin published Boccaccio's *Decameron*, and in 1739 Ariosto's comedy *Lena*. The anti-Jesuit satire *Pifferi di montagna che andarono per suonare e furono suonati* (1738), by 'Cesellio

---

[114] Salvino Salvini, *Postille all'opera del Negri*, Florence, Biblioteca Moreniana, MS 210, fol. 51ᵛ.

[115] The publisher Gaspero Ricci added the *Notizie* on Maltesti and Salvetti to his edition of *Le veglie piacevoli* (1759–83) by Domenico M. Manni, 'sembrandoci produzione ancor questa del nostro Autore, che bene spesso nella di lui gioventù fregiava l'Edizioni paterne con simili adornamenti' (*Le veglie piacevoli, ovvero notizie de' più bizzari e giocondi uomini Toscani, le quali possono servire di utile trattenimento: seconda edizione fiorentina*, 8 vols (Florence: Ricci, 1815–16), VI (1816), 114, n. 1).

[116] Cf. *Brindisi*, ed. by Manni, p. xviii. See Samuel Clegg, 'Thomas Hollis: Book-Lover, Politician, and Philanthropist', *The Bibliophile*, 1 (1908), 37–40 (p. 38).

[117] In the manuscript catalogue of the library of the Orto Botanico in Padua, we find the following record: 'Malatesti, Antonio, *La Tina, equivoci rusticali composti nel 1637 e dedicati a Giovanni Milton, copiati dall'originale ritrovato in Londra, con alcune notizie intorno all'Autore, raccolte da Gio. Lami*. MSS. in fogl. (Manoscritto di poesie non stampate, e inoltre pregevole per le notizie intorno l'autore, raccolte e mandate a Londra dal celebre D.ʳ Giov. Lami)': see 'Catalogo de' libri Marsili, trascrizione a cura di P. Mario', in *Il fondo Marsili nella biblioteca dell'orto botanico di Padova*, ed. by Alessandro Minelli, Alessandra Angarano, and Paola Mario (Treviso: Antilia, 2010), pp. 63–194 (p. 137, n. 1438).

[118] In the *Catalogue de la bibliothèque de M L***** (Paris: Maulde et Renou, 1847), Libri refers to the Edlin edition of these 'équivoques extrêmement libres [...] qui n'avaient jamais paru' (p. 256).

Filomastige', a possible pseudonym of Lami, appeared as printed by Edlin and Giovanni Pickard in Leida and London, but was actually printed in Florence.[119]

After the title page, the Edlin *Tina* has a short *Preface* in English which states that the text was based on Marsili's copy and that the *Notizie* 'are taken principally from memoirs furnished by the very learned and ingenious Dr. *Gio. Lami* of Florence'.[120] Additionally, on the verso of the title page there is a stanza which is wrongly attributed to Malatesti, but is drawn from Francini's ode (ll. 37–42) already prefaced to Milton's *Poems*, as correctly quoted in the Edinburgh manuscript.

In the fourth edition of his *Serie dei testi di lingua italiana*, the bibliographer and Crusca academician Bartolomeo Gamba claimed that the 1757 London editions of Malatesti's 'graziosissimi sonetti' were actually printed 'presso che 80 anni dopo in Venezia'.[121] The typesetting and the paper, which bears an Italian watermark, confirm that it is a later Italian edition, but there is more critical evidence to believe that *La Tina* was first published around 1837 and probably in Venice, which was at that time under Austrian censorship.

For a start, in his 1782 preface to the *Enimmi*, Rastrelli wrote that Malatesti 'lasciò molte opere manoscritte, degne certamente di star sepolte nell'oblìo per

---

[119] See Parenti, pp. 108–09; cf. Gaetano Melzi, *Dizionario di opere anonime e pseudonime di scrittori italiani o come che sia aventi relazione all'Italia*, 3 vols (Milan: Pirola, 1848–59), I (1848), 198.

[120] The adverb 'principally' may confirm that Lami's letter was not the first and only source of the *Notizie*. The beginning of the *Preface* to the Edlin edition reads as follows: 'This manuscript is presented to Dr. *John Marsili* of Venice, by *Thomas Hollis* of Lincoln's Inn. It is copied exactly after an original manuscript *in quarto*, found at a stall in London in this year 1757, by *Thomas Brand* Esq. of the Hide of Essex who generously bestowed it on his friend Mr. *Hollis*' (p. 5). Because of the punctuation some critics read 'copied by' instead of 'found by' Brand, e.g. Allodoli in his introduction to the aforementioned 1913 edition: 'Il manoscritto, venuto d'Inghilterra, e copiato dall'originale per opera di un signor Brand, fu regalato da costui a Giovanni Marsili' (p. viii). In the printed editions, the dedication to Milton has the following minor differences: 'Fiorentino' is added to the name of the author, and the sonnets are said to be 'Regalati' instead of 'Dedicati'.

[121] Bartolomeo Gamba, *Serie dei testi di lingua italiana e di altre opere importanti nella italiana letteratura dal secolo XIV al XIX*, 4th edn (Venice: Gondoliere, 1839), p. 551. According to Allodoli, this edition is 'una mistificazione dovuta al veneziano Giovanni Maneli, ed è invece stata stampata a Venezia 1837' (*Milton e l'Italia*, p. 32). There is another alleged London edition of *La Tina*, also in ottavo, which bears the only indication 'A spese dell'editore', *sine anno*, probably published by Gargano Gargini in Florence in 1859, as suggested by the author's entry in the catalogue sheet at the BNCF, Catalogo Palatino; cf. Fanfani, p. xxx. In the second part of the *Catalogue of the Mathematical, Historical, Bibliographical and Miscellaneous Portion of the Celebrated Library of M. Guglielmo Libri* (London: Sotheby, 1861), sold by Samuel L. Sotheby and John Wilkinson, we find an edition of *La Tina* in '8vo. Londra (Italia) a Spese dell'Editore', with the following note: 'The edition was limited to fifty copies on paper and four on vellum. It is very singular that such obscene sonnets should have been offered to Milton' (II, 485).

la loro troppo libera sfacciataggine', but among them 'molte se ne sono ritrovate piacevoli, e di brillante carattere rivestite; fra le quali alcuni sonetti equivoci rusticali, che forse verranno pubblicati'.[122] The 'rustic equivocal sonnets' are clearly those of *La Tina*, which therefore were not yet published by 1782. Another indication is provided by the anthology of *Poesie rusticali* published in 1808 by Giulio Ferrario, who mentions Malatesti's *Tina* not as a printed edition, as we would expect, but only as a manuscript kept in Magliabechi's library.[123]

In an 1853 bibliographical note, the critic and antiquary Bolton Corney argued that the only evidence for Gamba's claim laid in his 'authority', but he was nevertheless convinced that the place and date of publication were false, and suggested 'that Gamba himself was the editor of the volume', as shown by the fact that '*La Tina* appears under his name in the index'.[124] Gamba's involvement in the alleged London editions is most likely, as can be ascertained by a copy of the Edlin *Tina* which is included in the eighteenth volume of *Opuscoli Bassanesi* at the library of Bassano del Grappa, Gamba's birthplace in the province of Padua. This copy was presented by Gamba to the poet and fellow-citizen Giambattista Roberti, who wrote with a red pen on the inside of the back cover the following note: 'Stampato nella Tipogr. Alvisopoli per cura del Gamba scrittore della Notizia'.[125] The attribution of the *Notizia* to Gamba is, clearly, a mistaken assumption, but Roberti made sure that future readers could know the actual place and date of publication.

---

[122] Modesto Rastrelli, 'Breve notizia intorno alla vita d'Antonio Malatesti Fiorentino', in *Enimmi*, pp. 5–15 (p. 14).

[123] Giulio Ferrario, *Poesie pastorali e rusticali, raccolte ed illustrate, con note* (Milan: Società Tipografica de' Classici Italiani, 1808), p. xix, n. 2: 'Nella Magliabecchiana esiste un manoscritto della *Tina* di Antonio Malatesti, ossia raccolta di cinquanta sonetti rusticali, e presso l'eruditissimo Sig. Marchese Giuseppe Pucci di Firenze, che con somma gentilezza mi ha comunicato non poche delle suddette notizie, esiste un Idillio Rusticale inedito del Senatore Vincenzo Alamanni morto non è gran tempo, intitolato *Lamento di Cencio dell'Antella* composto nel 1763'. He clearly refers to the aforementioned copy of *La Tina* now classed Magl. VII. 1356, which may suggest that the Alamanni-attribution could be to Vincenzo, instead of Andrea, exactly because of this confusion: the copy arrived to La Crusca in 1762, and Alamanni's 'rustic' poem dates just one year later.

[124] Bolton Corney, 'Milton and Malatesti', *Notes and Queries*, 202 (1853), 237–38 (p. 238). Cf. Gamba, p. 766. Parenti simply reports: 'Un'edizione curata a Venezia dal Gamba, su una copia ms. portata da Londra dal Prof. Marsili di Padova' (p. 117).

[125] A collation with other publications by Alvisopoli, managed by Gamba until 1836 and then by his son Francesco, would give further evidence: for example, the *Dicerie di Annibal Caro e di altri a' re della Virtù* (1538), edited by Gamba and allegedly published by 'Calveley-Hall', was printed in Venice by Alvisopoli in 1821 (see Parenti, p. 44), and its uneven cut of paper is the same of the supposed Edlin edition of *La Tina*; the typesetting of the *Lettera discorsiva* on the Palazzo Ducale of Venice, written by Pietro Bettio and printed by Alvisopoli in 1837, is the same of the printed *Tina*.

After Hollis's death, historical traces of the original manuscript of *La Tina* are sparse. All we know is that the Brand-Hollis library was inherited by Reverend John Disney, and auctioned after his death by Samuel Sotheby in London in 1817.[126] Malatesti's rustic equivocations found their way into the 'curious and splendid' collection of the Member of Parliament George Watson Taylor. The manuscript was sold again on 15 April 1823 by the auctioneer Robert Harding Evans in Pall-Mall, with the help of the Scottish publisher George Nicol, and the catalogue of sales confirms that it was already 'bound in green morocco'.[127] It was probably on this occasion that Reverend Henry John Todd saw the manuscript, as he wrote about it in the third edition of his *Life of Milton*.[128]

Evans' auction was also attended by the literary scholar Samuel Weller Singer. He was the last person who reported on the original manuscript of *La Tina*, which he considered 'interesting as a monument of the respect and attention' that Milton received in Florence; with permission of the dealer, he copied eight sonnets and the 'inscribed stone tablet' representing the salient dedication to Milton, but for some reason he only published his notes about thirty years later, in 1850.[129] He did not know that there was a printed edition and was not able to provide any further information about the current location, or even existence, of the manuscript.

When *La Tina* was printed, the 1637 manuscript was in fact already in Edinburgh. The long scholarly oversight of this manuscript is almost ironic, considering that Masson was a professor at the University of Edinburgh in 1859, when he added a substantial footnote on it to the revised first volume of his *Life of Milton*.[130] So far, we can only speculate on hypotheses about the acquisition by the Advocates Library, but we can take Evans's sale in 1823 as a *terminus a quo* and set the *terminus ante quem* around the year 1830, when the Advocates' Faculty Record, which contains the *Poetry Catalogue* with the first entry of *La Tina*, was closed.[131]

---

[126] The MS was probably purchased by the bookseller Robert Triphook: see *A Catalogue of the Very Valuable and Highly Interesting United Libraries of Thomas Hollis, Esq. and Thomas Brand Hollis* (1817), in *Sale Catalogues of Libraries of Eminent Persons*, 12 vols (London: Mansell, 1971–75), VIII: *Politicians* (1973), p. 46.

[127] Robert H. Evans, *Catalogue of the Choice, Curious, and Splendid London Library of George Watson Taylor, Esq. M.P. Part the Second* (London: Nicol, 1823), p. 12, n. 268.

[128] Henry J. Todd, *Some Account of the Life and Writings of John Milton, Derived Principally from Documents in His Majesty's State-Paper Office*, 3rd edn (London: Rivington, 1826), pp. 33–34.

[129] Samuel W. Singer, 'Dedication to Milton by Antonio Malatesti', *Notes and Queries*, 40 (1850), 146–47 (p. 146). In a second note, Singer commented: these sonnets 'are certainly very ingenious, and may be "graziosissimi" to an Italian ear and imagination; but I cannot think that the pure mind of Milton would take much delight in obscene allusions, however neatly wrapped up' ('Milton and Malatesti', *Notes and Queries*, 204 (1853), 295–96 (p. 295)).

[130] Masson, pp. 735–36.

A cognate manuscript in the Advocates Library, originally held at the Signet Library in Edinburgh, is a *Raccolta di poesie in lingua rusticana padovana* by various authors of the seventeenth century.[132] This manuscript formerly belonged to the Paduan Dominican Alberto Zaramellini and comes from the library of Frederick North, Fifth Earl of Guilford, which was largely sold by Evans from 1828 to 1830. Lord Guilford's collection of books and manuscripts shows an extensive interest in Italian poetry, including an original copy of Tasso's *Gerusalemme liberata* in the author's handwriting,[133] and includes many items of the Paduan rustic tradition, for example *Le Rime in lingua rustica padovana, con una tradottione del primo Canto de Ariosto* (1558) and a number of works by the 'famosissimo Ruzante', namely the Paduan playwright Angelo Beolco.[134]

When not part of bequests or individual gifts, the books of the Advocates Library were bought after recommendation by the Committee of Curators. The main literary acquisitions were in the field of ancient and modern criticism, 'but very little poetry',[135] and it is precisely in this connection that we may assume Walter Scott's interest, if not his direct involvement. Considering that the great 'Unknown Author of *Waverley*' was appointed member of the bibliophile Roxburghe Club in 1823,[136] namely in the same year that Watson Taylor sold the manuscript of *La Tina*, it is unlikely that Sir Walter did not know about it. It seems equally implausible that he purchased the manuscript himself, but he could

---

[131] In the *Poetry Catalogue* (NLS, FR 190) *La Tina* is recorded as '4to 30 leaves', but the bound MS is smaller than octavo. Neither Malatesti nor *La Tina* appears in the Register of Books Purchased (1818–37). The Advocates' librarian between 1820 and 1848 was David Irving.

[132] NLS, Adv. MS 19. 3. 39. In 1805–37, the librarian of the Signet Library was Macvey Napier, who enriched the Signet collection with many foreign books and manuscripts; unfortunately, the catalogue of books purchased between 1823 and 1830 is currently missing. However, the Paduan *Raccolta* is marked with the initial 'L', possibly the antiquarian and bookseller David Laing, who succeeded to Napier in 1837 after failing to be appointed to the librarianship of the Advocates' Library in 1820, despite support from Sir Walter; the NLS *Poetry Catalogue* was largely compiled by Laing, and it is possible that he was involved in the purchase of *La Tina*; see George H. Ballantyne, *The Signet Library Edinburgh and its Librarians, 1722–1972* (Glasgow: Scottish Library Association, 1979), pp. 18–19.

[133] See Anna Jameson, *A Handbook to the Public Galleries of Art in and Near London*, 2 vols (London: Murray, 1842), II, 562.

[134] See Robert H. Evans, *Catalogue of the Valuable and Extensive Library of the Late Earl of Guilford* (London, 1828–29), pp. 28 and 35. On the important tradition of rustic poetry in the Paduan vernacular, see Gianfranco Contini, 'La poesia rusticale come caso di bilinguismo', in *La poesia rusticana nel Rinascimento: Atti del Convegno* (Rome: Accademia Nazionale dei Lincei, 1969), pp. 43–55; now in *Ultimi esercizî ed elzeviri* (Turin: Einaudi, 1989), pp. 6–21.

[135] John B. St. Clair and Roger Craik, *The Advocates Library: 300 Years of a National Institution 1689–1989* (Edinburgh: HMSO, 1989), p. 27.

[136] See George Allan, *Life of Sir Walter Scott: With Critical Notices of his Writings* (Edinburgh: Ireland Jr., 1834), p. 443. In March 1828, Watson Taylor sent to the Advocates Library an English copy of poems by Charles d'Orléans, which he had recently presented to the Roxburghe Club (see NLS, FR 339e(i)/49). On 7 May 1828, Scott recorded in his journal: 'Dined at

well have recommended it to the curators of the Advocates Library or to the librarians of the Signet. Not only did he read Italian literature widely, but in his library at Abbotsford he kept the edition of *Rusticali dei primi tre secoli* and other pastoral and dithyrambic poems which are closely related in genre and style to Malatesti's 'rustic equivocations',[137] as we shall see in the following section.

4. The Genre of 'La Tina': A New Rustic Style

The first of Malatesti's equivocal sonnets addressed to Tina is probably the one contained in a notebook dated 1630, simply entitled *Equivoco I*: 'Da poi ch'io servo teco per zimbello'.[138] The 'zimbello' is a little bird used as a decoy, but also denotes, as explained by Galilei in a humourous *postilla*, 'alcuni piccoli sacchetti pieni di crusca legati in capo di una cordicella, coi quali i nostri fattori il carnevale soglion sacchettare e zimbellare le maschere',[139] and by figurative extension an object of mockery, a laughing stock. In Malatesti's equivocal sonnet, the verb 'servire' further entails a satire against the topos of *servitium amoris*, with predictable sodomitic connotations, as confirmed for example by the first tercet of Sonnet xxx, *Sopra il versar della botte*:

> Ti turerò ogni buco ed ogni fesso,
> o Tina, in carità, perch'io non faccio
> questi servizi mai per interesse. (ll. 9–11)

The *Equivoco I* is crossed out and was not transcribed in the 1637 collection dedicated to Milton, but is included in the 1650 manuscript dedicated to Cordini. The exclusion of this sonnet from the earlier collection may be motivated by issues about the authorship of other manuscript works in the same genre as *La Tina*. In fact, this sonnet is directly related to the beginning of a rustic poem attributed to Jacopo Cicognini, which was first printed in the 1788 collection of *Rusticali dei*

Mr. Watson Taylor's' (*The Journal of W. Scott, from the Original Manuscript at Abbotsford*, 2 vols (New York: Harper & Brothers, 1891), II, p. 173).

[137] *Rusticali dei primi tre secoli* is vol. xxxiii (1788) of *Parnaso italiano*, ed. by Andrea Rubbi, 56 vols (Venice: Zatta, 1784–91). See the *Catalogue of the Library at Abbotsford* (Edinburgh: Constable, 1838). Probably during his last Italian tour, Scott also purchased a copy of *La Cinthia, favola boscareccia* (Naples: Salviani, 1594), written by Carlo Noci after Tasso's *Aminta*, which was one of the direct sources of *The Queenes Arcadia* (1606) by Samuel Daniel.

[138] *Poesie di Antonio Malatesti*, BNCF, Magl. VII. 231, fol. 31ʳ. See Masieri, pp. 49–50. Another MS notebook, Magl. VII. 220, contains a canzone so far unpublished entitled *Alla Tina*: 'Staman nella mia ragna | qua sotto Calenzano | io trovai quell'uccel ch'ha il capo rosso. | Senti come si lagna | e beccami la mano. | Tina, che farebb'ei se fusse grosso? | Tener più non lo posso | perch'egli è tutto rabbia | e il caso non mi par da porlo in gabbia. | Onde a fartene un dono | risoluto mi sono, | e se svolazza e grida | quando ti par l'uccida | forse che a te sarà più accetto e grato | s'è di tua man pelato' (fol. 401ʳ).

[139] Galilei, *Opere*, VI (1896), 381, n. 10.

primi tre secoli, that is to say *Pippo lavoratore da Legnaja*: 'Dopo ch'i' ho servito per zimbello'.[140] There is evidence, however, that this rustic stanzas were also composed by Malatesti. In the last octave of *Il Cecco da Scandicci mandato via contra tempo dal Podere*, which circulated anonymously in manuscript form until print publication in 1666, Malatesti is clearly portrayed as the author, together with his *Sfinge* and a rustic poem entitled *Pippo*;[141] and in the *Dialogo di un Poeta e di uno Scapigliato*, Malatesti mentions, among his works, that 'nel Pippo vi son dei bei capricci | e così nel tuo Cecco da Scandicci'.[142]

Malatesti's friendship with Jacopo's son may provide another clue. Giacinto was still a schoolboy when he published his first book, *Descrizione del corso al palio de' villani* (1619), and this volume also contained a number of *Stanze di Cecco alla Tina*.[143] It is possible, then, that the later inclusion of *Equivoco I* in the 1650 *Tina* depended on Malatesti's decision to claim the authorship of *Pippo*, as he did with the final octave added to his *Cecco*, shortly after the untimely death of Giacinto in 1649.[144] We may safely infer, at least, that it was within the familial circle of the Cicogninis that Malatesti's *Tina* was initially conceived.

In order to better appreciate the genre of *La Tina*, we should consider more closely the names of the peasant poet and his rustic muse. Sears suggested that 'Nencio' is 'the Florentine dialect form of *nuncio* ("messenger")', which would be interesting in so far as it would create another playful allusion to Galileo; but this is rather an interpretive pun.[145] The name derives by aphaeresis and

---

[140] See *Pippo lavoratore da Legnaja: alle Dame Fiorentine. Stanze rusticali* and *Allegrezza di Pippo per la nascita del primo figliuolo: stanze rusticali*, in *Rusticali dei primi tre secoli*, pp. 41–48; also in *Poemetti contadineschi*, ed. by Massimo Bontempelli (Carabba: Lanciano, 1914), pp. 88–99.

[141] *Il Cecco da Scandicci, mandato via contrattempo dal Podere: alle bellissime Dame* (Florence: Stamperia di S.A.S., 1666); see Negri, p. 63; cf. Melzi, II, 345. At the National Libraries of Florence and Rome there are two anonymous copies of a *zingana* — i.e. a Tuscan rustic comedy in the style of gipsy songs (see Salvini, *Discorsi*, III, 107) — entitled *La Tina sposa di due, cioè, di Cecco e di Maso* (Padova [Florence: Bolli], s.d.); the author could be the Florentine Apatista Giovanni Battista Fagiuoli, as suggested by a note at the end of the Roman copy: see BNCF, MS Th. 4. E. 88, and Rome, Biblioteca Nazionale Centrale, MS 35. 9. I. 17. 3.

[142] See Neri, p. 106. In his 1782 preface to the *Enimmi*, Rastrelli had already noted that among other works by Malatesti, 'furono stampati due Opuscoletti Rusticali, l'uno intitolato: *Il Cecco da Scandicci mandato via contrattempo dal Podere*, e l'altro *Pippo da Legnaja*, i quali opuscoli son rarissimi per essere in foglio volante' (p. 13).

[143] Giacinto A. Cicognini, *Descrizione del Corso al Palio de' Villani trasformati in Civettoni* (Florence: Cecconcelli, 1619). On the rustic stanzas *Alla Tina*, see Negri, p. 237, and Ferrario, p. xiii, n. 1. In Libri's *Catalogue of the Extraordinary Collection of Splendid Manuscripts* (London: Davy and Sons, 1859), there is an entry for *Rime di diversi autori* (Lamberti, Ruspoli, J.A. Cicognini, Giraldi, Villafranchi, Malatesti, &c.), with the following comment: 'Most of these poems, written in Florence, are of a free character and unpublished' (p. 254).

[144] See Flavia Cancedda and Silvia Castelli, *Per una bibliografia di Giacinto Andrea Cicognini* (Florence: Alinea, 2001), pp. 63–64. Cf. Italiano Marchetti, 'Note sulla poesia rusticale', *Studi secenteschi*, 1 (1960), 61–81 (pp. 75–77).

regressive assimilation from 'Lorenzo', and came to signify 'a foole, an idiot, a naturall', as noted by John Florio in his 1611 *Dictionarie*.[146] More relevantly, the name of the fictional peasant poet signals the tradition of the *Nencia da Barberino*, a 'poemetto rusticano' in fifty octaves probably composed before 1470 and traditionally attributed to Lorenzo de' Medici, but also credited to Lorenzo's court poet Bernardo Giambullari.[147] The literary historian Francesco De Sanctis described quite well the Boccaccesque 'tono equivoco' of the *Nencia*, whose nuanced equivocations could be read as 'a page of the *Decameron*'.[148]

La Nencia opened a rich popular vein in Tuscan poetry. It marked the beginning of 'un genere nuovo e tutto fiorentino', as emphasized by the historian of popular literature Alessandro D'Ancona.[149] Another one of Lorenzo's court poets, the aforementioned Pulci, first parodied it with the stanzas dedicated to *La Beca di Dicomano*, composed immediately after 1470, whose first octave precisely begins by complaining about Nencia's overstated fame.[150] In turn, Bartolomeo Del Bene began the second octave of his later *Stanze di Meo di Valdelsa alla Tina da Campi* as follows: 'La Tina mia è più bella che sette | Nencie,

---

[145] Sears, p. 281; the translator also suggests that Nencio 'seems to be Malatesti's pseudonym for himself in the role of a small farmer' (p. 313, n. 19).

[146] John Florio, *Queen Anna's New World of Words* (London: Bradwood and Stansby, 1611; facsimile repr. Menston: Scolar Press, 1968), p. 331.

[147] See Alberto Chiari and Italiano Marchetti, *L'autore della 'Nencia da Barberino'* (Milan: Marzorati, 1948). Cf. Arnaldo Di Benedetto, 'Due note sulla "Nencia da Barberino"', in *La poesia rusticana*, pp. 29–41. Under the pseudonym 'Biagio del Capperone', Giambullari was also author of several tailed sonnets in 'stile rusticale', many of which had lively obscene double-entendres: see *Sonetti rusticani di Biagio del Capperone*, ed. by Costantino Arlìa (Città di Castello: Lapi, 1902). In the 'ottave rusticali per la maternità della Nencia', also allegedly by Giambullari, the name of Nencia's daughter is 'Bettina' (BML, MS Ashburnham 419, fol. 68), and Malatesti composed a comedy in octaves entitled *La Betta*, which we can read together with *La Tina da Castello* in BNCF, MS Magl.VII. 233, fols 57ʳ–67ʳ.

[148] Francesco De Sanctis, *Storia della letteratura italiana* (1870–71), trans. by Joan Redfern, *History of Italian Literature*, 2 vols (London: Milford (Oxford University Press), 1930), I, 395. In 1750 Baretti also composed some 'stanze contadinesche' entitled *La Nencia*: see *Le piacevoli poesie* (Turin: Stamperia Reale, 1750), now in *Opere di Giuseppe Baretti scritte in lingua italiana*, 5 vols (Milan: Mussi, 1814), IV, 98–103; Baretti sent a copy of his 'sguaiatissime rime' enclosed with a letter to Lami dated 20 May 1750, and explained: 'Ella troverà in questo mio libricciolo alcune rime in lingua rustica fiorentina. Gli è impossibile che sien buone, ché io non sono mai stato in Toscana, e pochissime cose scritte abbiamo stampate in tal genere ch'io sappia' (*Epistolario*, ed. by Luigi Piccioni, 2 vols (Bari: Laterza, 1936), I, 91–92).

[149] Alessandro D'Ancona, *La poesia popolare italiana* (Livorno: Vigo, 1878), p. 128. Together with Ferrario's *Poesie pastorali e rusticali*, many poems of this genre can also be found in *Rime burlesche di eccellenti autori*, ed. by Pietro Fanfani (Florence: Le Monnier, 1856), which includes Malatesti's octaves *La compagnia di Belfiore*.

[150] Luigi Pulci, *La Beca*, in *Opere minori*, ed. by Paolo Orvieto (Milan: Mursia, 1986), pp. 133–50: 'Ognun la Nencia tutta notte canta | e della Beca non se ne ragiona' (p. 133). *La Beca* was first

e più vaga che cinquanta Beche'.[151] At last, in the octaves of *Ravanello alla Nenciotta* (1626) by Francesco Bracciolini, one of the creators of the mock-heroic poem, the peasant lover-poet is ironically called 'radish'.[152] Among other 'erotic idylls', Nencio will also feature in the *Lamento di Cecco da Varlungo* (1694), by Francesco Baldovini, later reworked by Fiacchi in his *Lamento in morte della Sandra* (1804), which elaborates on an 'amorazzo contadino' from Boccaccio's *Decameron* (VIII. 2).[153]

Like Nencio, the name of the rustic muse is also susceptible to double reading, and points towards another seminal work in which *La Tina* is inscribed for its genre. On the one hand, at a literal level, the word 'tina' is the feminine variant of 'tino' and simply denotes 'a vat, a great vessel were grapes are pressed to make wine', as Baretti noted in his *Dizionario*.[154] As such, 'Tina' made an ideal name for rustic and dithyrambic poetry without classicist pretensions, and was generically used in Tuscan poetry to denote a country woman, for example in Lippi's *Malmantile* (XII. 1. 3). We also find the 'villanella' Tina in *La Tancia* (1611), a popular 'commedia rusticale' by Michelangelo Buonarroti the Young, nephew *ex fratre* of the great painter, sculptor and poet.[155] As a short form of 'Caterina', on the other hand, *Tina* relates to the burlesque comedy *La Catrina* (c. 1517), composed by the young Francesco Berni during his years in Florence.[156]

---

printed in 1568 together with *La Nencia*, then re-published in 1759 with sonnets by Matteo Franco, another amateur poet at Lorenzo's court, from an original manuscript owned by Dati (see Gamba, p. 147).

[151] Bartolomeo Del Bene, *Stanze di Meo di Valdelsa alla Tina da Campi*, in *Poesie varie*, BNCF, MS Magl. VII. 446, fols 4ʳ–9ᵛ. The first print edition is in *Rime* (Livorno: Poggiali, 1799 [1816]); see also *Un idillio rusticale e altre rime valdelsane*, ed. by Nello Tarchiani (Castelfiorentino: Società Storica della Valdelsa, 1903).

[152] Bracciolini's *Nenciotta* was first published as an appendix to the second edition of his main mock-heroic poem, *Lo scherno degli dei* (Rome: Mascardi, 1626). See Guido Arbizzoni, 'Poesia epica, eroicomica, satirica, burlesca. La poesia rusticale toscana. La poesia figurata', in *Storia della letteratura italiana*, dir. by Enrico Malato, 14 vols (Rome: Salerno Editrice, 1995–2004), v: *La fine del Cinquecento e il Seicento* (1997), 727–70.

[153] See Francesco Baldovini, *I lamenti di Cecco da Varlungo*, ed. by Olga S. Casale (Rome: Salerno Editrice, 1991). The 1755 edition of Baldovini's *Lamento* (Florence: Stamperia Moückiana) was prefaced with a sonnet by Bartolommeo Del Teglia dedicated to 'Firmelto' (i.e. Orazio Marrini), 'Accademico Fiorentino e Segretario dell'Accademia degli Apatisti', who richly annotated the poem.

[154] Giuseppe Baretti, *A Dictionary of the English and Italian Languages*, 2 vols (London: Richardson, 1760), I, 678; cf. Florio, p. 564: 'any kind of tunne or great vat'. See *La Tina*'s Sonnet XLIV, *Sopra la bigoncia*: 'L'uva e già ghezza, e sono in molle i tini'; cf. Sonnet XIX, *Sopra l'imbottare*.

[155] Interestingly, the name of the author was only revealed in the second edition of this comedy, published in Florence in 1638, namely about one year after Malatesti's *Tina* (see Ferrario, p. 22). Cecco is a protagonist of this comedy, and the name Nencio also occurs.

With its taste for plurilingualism and its burlesque use of Dantesque *terza rima*, poetry 'alla bernesca' became the main style of modern anti-classicism. Its two main sources were the ludic vein of Lorenzo's carnival songs and the mordant *vituperia* by Domenico di Giovanni, called 'il Burchiello'.[156] Its influence has spanned the centuries. Even a 'neo-classical' poet like Giacomo Leopardi composed Bernesque verse, and in one of the many insightful notes of his *Zibaldone* he wrote that 'le poesie rusticali come la *Nencia*, *Cecco da Varlungo* ec.' are the authentic Theocrytean idylls of early modern Italy, which effectively rival their classical model in that they are 'più burleschi'.[158]

There is clearly a wider social context to be considered in relation to the development of Tuscan rustic poetry. During the sixteenth century the aristocracy largely colonized the countryside, converting the 'rusticali abituri' used by the peasants into more civilized 'villas'.[159] As a consequence, the traditional opposition between *urbs* and *contado* was being re-defined too. While the aristocracy developed the idyllic sense of a lost harmony with nature, it also relished the so far 'minor' tradition of rustic poetry in the vernacular, setting the ideal stage for the poetics of the seventeenth century. It was 'during this despicable period of exhausted repose', Vernon Lee pointed out, 'that took place the partial renovation which produced the modern Italian world'.[160] The Apatista poet Orazio Ricasoli-Rucellai, who pretended to be a pupil of Galileo, exhorted his reader: 'Lascia la corte per la villa'.[161]

The new relationship between city and countryside can be further illustrated by Galileo. Not only did the astronomer think 'che la città fosse in certo modo la

---

[156] *La Catrina* was first published posthumously (Florence: Panizzi, 1567). See F. Berni, *Le Rime e La Catrina*, ed. by Fernando Palazzi (Rome: Formiggini, 1915).

[157] According to the rhetorician Antonio Minturno, it was more precisely Ariosto that 'mostrò potersi la Satyrica materia attamente scrivere con terzetti': *L'Arte poetica* (Venice: Valvassori, 1563), p. 276. Berni adopted the same metrical form, but with a burlesque-parodistic intent, rather than a didactic-satyrical one: see Uberto Limentani, *La satira nel Seicento* (Milan: Ricciardi 1961), p. 2. Buonarroti's *Satira prima* may offer a good example of the connection between carnivalesque and rustic poetry: 'Or ch'è 'n su lo 'ngrassarsi il carnovale, | [...] Tornate a rivestirvi il rusticale' (*Opere varie in versi ed in prose*, ed. by P. Fanfani (Florence: Le Monnier, 1863), p. 219).

[158] Giacomo Leopardi, *Zibaldone* (1817–32), in *Tutte le opere*, ed. Walter Binni and Enrico Ghidetti, 2 vols (Florence: Sansoni, 1969), II, 57.

[159] Francesco Inghirami, *Storia della Toscana, compilata ed in sette epoche distribuita*, 16 vols (Fiesole: Poligrafia Fiesolana, 1843), IX (1843), 248. In a famous 1513 letter, Niccolò Machiavelli describes his daily life in a farm outside Florence with the words 'Io mi sto in villa', as opposed to the life of the city: see *Lettere*, ed. by Franco Gaeta, in *Opere*, 3 vols (Turin: UTET, 1984), III, 424.

[160] Vernon Lee, *Studies in the Eighteenth Century in Italy* (London: Satchell, 1880), p. 11.

[161] *Poesie di diversi autori del XVII*, BNCF, MS Palat. 263, fol. 25 (see D'Afflitto, p. 154). Dati's *censura* was precisely of a sonnet by Ricasoli-Rucellai, as explained by Fiacchi (pseud. Clasio): see *Collezione d'opuscoli scientifici e letterari ed estratti d'opere interressanti*, 22 vols (Florence:

prigione degl'ingegni speculativi, e che la libertà della campagna fosse il libro della natura, sempre aperto', as related by Viviani;[162] his confinement in Arcetri was also naturally 'conducive to poetry', as Eric Cochrane commented: 'Hence the excitement when a real live "peasant poet" — and not just one of Antonio Malatesti's imaginary rustic "verse distillers" — was discovered near Arcidosso'.[163] We may think of it as a period of poetic 'rustication' for Galileo, but not really in the Miltonian sense: the vernacular of the countryside was not the pure Tuscan of Monsignor Giovanni Della Casa, which Milton strived to imitate — and let us not forget that Della Casa also composed Bernesque verse, in particular during his attendance of the Roman Academy of the 'Vignaioli'.[164] Galileo himself was 'a burlesque and easy poet', as Baretti called him,[165] and enjoyed reading Berni as much as Petrarch;[166] his biographer Niccolò Gherardini tells us that Galileo 'spesso havea in bocca i capitoli del Berni', and that he took 'gran piacere' in the work of Ruzante, whose rustic and equivocal comedies, like *La Betía* (1523-25), so vividly contrasted with the idealized world of Jacopo Sannazaro's *Arcadia* (1504).[167]

With the paradoxical encomiums of his *capitoli* in praise of all 'things of naught' and 'naughty things', as Anthony Oldcorn put it, Bernesque poetry also epitomized an early modern climax of 'homosexual humanism'.[168] For example, given Berni's notoriously equivocal use of 'needle' as a phallic metaphor in his *Capitolo dell'ago* — which was 'recited' by the author and largely reconstructed

---

Stamperia di Borgo Ognissanti, 1807-18), XI (1810), 64. Cf. Quinto Marini, 'Barocco in villa: le ingegnose Arcadie del Seicento', in *I Capricci di Proteo: Percorsi e linguaggi del Barocco*, ed. by Bruno Basile and others (Rome: Salerno Editrice, 2002), pp. 333-77.

[162] Viviani, p. 625. Galileo's disciple was also a member of the Apatisti (see Benevenuti, p. 257).

[163] Cochrane, p. 226. The 'peasant poet' was Giovanni Domenico Peri; as an example of 'simple and healthy' country life, however, Cochrane ironically quotes Malatesti's Sonnet v, *Sopra l'arista e la salsiccia* (ibid.).

[164] See Antonio Corsaro, 'Giovanni Della Casa e la poesia burlesca', in *La regola e la licenza: studi sulla poesia satirica e burlesca fra Cinque e Seicento* (Rome: Vecchiarelli, 1999), pp. 73-113.

[165] Giuseppe Baretti, *The Italian Library: Containing an Account of the Lives and Works of the Most Valuable Authors of Italy* (London: Millar, 1757), p. 52.

[166] As Viviani reports, Galileo knew by heart 'quasi tutto il Petrarca' and 'tutte le rime del Berni' (p. 627).

[167] Niccolò Gherardini, *Vita di Galileo Galilei celebre Matematico, e Nobile Patrizio Fiorentino* (1654), in Galilei, *Opere*, XIX, 633-46 (pp. 644-45). See Ruzante, 'La Betía', in *Teatro: prima edizione completa*, ed. and trans. by Ludovico Zorzi (Turin: Einaudi, 1967), pp. 143-509; see also Angelo Beolco (il Ruzante), *La prima oratione*, ed. by Linda. L. Carroll (London: MHRA, 2009). Cf. Ronnie Ferguson, 'Explorations of Genre and Language', in *The Theatre of Angelo Beolco (Ruzante): Text, Context and Performance* (Ravenna: Longo, 2000), pp. 121-61.

[168] Anthony Oldcorn, 'The Anti-Classicist Tradition: Parody, Satire, Burlesque', in *CHIL*, pp. 268-76 (p. 270). Salvator Rosa called this sort of burlesque *encomia* 'frascherie da sezzo', and asked rhetorically: 'Lodar le Mosche, i Grilli, il Ravanello | E l'altre scioccherie ch'hanno composto | Il Bernia, il Mauro, il Lasca et il Borchiello?' (*Poesie e lettere edite e inedite di Salvator Rosa*, 2 vols (Naples: Tipografia della Regia Università, 1892), I, 199).

from memory by some of his followers –,[169] we can imagine the reaction of the Florentine academic audience to Milton's recital of the last two verses of his Sonnet VI: 'Sol troverete in tal parte men duro | Ove amor mise l'insanabil ago'.[170] This is where Malatesti's dedication may well have hit the mark. Just as Milton's masque in praise of chastity, *Comus*, can be contextualized against the backdrop of the 'Castlehaven scandal' — in which the Second Earl of Castlehaven was indicted, and eventually beheaded in 1631 'for raping his own wife and committing sodomy with one of his servants', possibly called 'Florence' –,[171] Malatesti set his erotic equivocations in the heart of the Florentine pastoral scene, as Singer commented quoting the rustic love from Tibullus's *Elegiae*: 'Ipsa Venus latos iam nunc migravit in agros' (II. 3. 3).[172]

More to the point of Malatesti's work, in the burlesque vocabulary the diminutive form 'tinella' is used as a metaphorical substitute for the female sexual organ, and the poet plays on this equivocal term in Sonnet XLVIII (*Sopra il far l'olio*). In the first modern history of comic verse, namely the *Ragionamento sopra la poesia giocosa* by Nicola Villani (1590–1636), which outlines the history of the genre from the 'poesia fallica' of ancient Greece, the author mentions the word 'tinella' as a meaningless expression coined by the Greek poet Archilochus 'per imitare il suono che la cetra faceva di Polifemo', and notes that it was still used by Tuscan poets.[173]

The idea of Tuscan peasants reciting tercets while ploughing the fields is, of course, a cliché; but it is safe to say that the lively tradition of Tuscan rustic songs, like the *maggiolate* in Sonnet XL (*Sopra il sonar il cembalo*), added to the general aspiration of reviving the musical sources of Greek poetry, as envisioned by the Florentine Camerata towards the creation of opera,[174] and not insignificantly through the renewal of dithyrambic songs, which remained seemingly

---

[169] See Brian Richardson, '"Recitato e cantato": the Oral Diffusion of Lyric Poetry in Sixteenth-Century Italy', in *Theatre, Opera, and Performance in Italy from the Fifteenth Century to the Present: Essays in Honour of Richard Andrews*, ed. by Brian Richardson, Simon Gilson, and Catherine Keen (Egham: Society for Italian Studies, 2004), pp. 67–82 (p. 76).

[170] *Minor Poems*, p. 58. See F. Berni, *Rime*, ed. by Danilo Romei (Milan: Mursia, 1985), pp. 58–61. Toscan comments: 'L'aiguille est avant tout un instrument cylindrique et pointu: par ces deux qualités, elle se prête à symboliser le phallus et, dans la littérature burlesque, le phallus spécialisé' (*CDL*, III, 1289); see the textile metaphors and the play on 'la crusca' in Sonnet VIII, *Sopra il tessere*.

[171] Barbara Breasted, '*Comus* and the Castlehaven Scandal', *Milton Studies*, 3 (1971), 201–24 (p. 203). Cf. Leah S. Marcus, 'John Milton's *Comus*', in *A Companion to Milton*, ed. by Thomas N. Corns (Malden, MA: Blackwell, 2001), pp. 232–45. Cynthia B. Herrup comments that the Earl's association with Catholicism 'tapped into the long-imagined association among the Roman Church, Italy, and sodomy' (*A House in Gross Disorder: Sex, Law, and the 2nd Earl of Castlehaven* (Oxford: Oxford University Press, 1999), p. 37); see also Robert Entzminger, 'The politics of love in Tasso's *Aminta* and Milton's *Comus*', in Di Cesare, pp. 463–76.

[172] 'Milton and Malatesti', pp. 295–96.

[173] *Ragionamento dello Accademico Aldeano* [Nicola Villani] *sopra la poesia giocosa de' Greci, de' Latini, e de' Toscani: con alcune poesie piacevoli del medesimo autore* (Venice: Pinelli, 1634), p. 50.

inconsequential in Latin poetry. Among the Palatini manuscripts in Florence there is, for example, a 'dialogo rusticale' which 'parrebbe fatto per esser cantato a ballo nella fine della *Catrina* del Berni', as described by Luigi Gentile.[175]

De Sanctis captured the new poetics of the 'scrittori melodrammatici', from Tasso to Giambattista Marino, with the following epigrammatic sentence: 'Literature was dying, and music was being born'.[176] Unlike Tasso's *Aminta*, however, Malatesti did not even attempt to fine-tune his 'rustiche sampogne'.[177] Sonnnet 1 sets out to 'metter la poesia in canzona', namely to make poetry sing, but with persiflage.

If one of the main founders of the Academy of Arcadia, Giovan Mario Crescimbeni, exemplified the importance of phonetic 'intercalari' precisely with Villani's use of 'Tina tinella',[178] the aforementioned copy of *La Tina* made by Fiacchi shows an obvious interest of the Arcadians in Tuscan rustic verse. In this respect, it can be argued that the rustic genre represents an essential link between the early modern 'favole pastorali' and the Arcadian project of poetic restoration, a project which lies within the Tuscan tradition and without the radical disruption of the linguistic model represented by Petrarch's *Canzoniere*.[179] Coltellini's academy has contributed largely to this tradition.[180]

As a representative instance of this link, in 1652 Cardinal Leopoldo De' Medici presented Christina Queen of Sweden with an anthology of poems by Malatesti,

---

[174] See *The Florentine Camerata: Documentary Studies and Translations*, ed. by Claude V. Palisca (New Haven: Yale University Press, 1989). See also Angelo Solerti, *Musica, ballo e drammatica alla corte Medicea dal 1600 al 1637* (Florence: Bemporad, 1905; repr. Bologna: Forni, 1969).

[175] BNCF, MS Palat. 251; see *I Codici Palatini*, ed. by L. Gentile, 2 vols (Rome: Presso i principali librai, 1889), I, p. 393, n. 39; cf. Marchetti, pp. 82–85. The MS anthology Palat. 274 also includes a sonnet by Francesco Melosio, *Ho inteso, Tina, ch'esclamando vai* (II, 121), followed by other sonnets by Malatesti, one of which, the sonnet *Signora mia, voi la pensate male* (p. 124; Gentile, p. 483, XI. 2), is also attributed to Melosio (cf. Gentile, p. 423, XXXI. 1).

[176] De Sanctis, II, 710. John Addington Symonds likewise commented: 'Great tragedy and great comedy were denied to the Italians. But they produced a novel species in the pastoral drama, which testified to their artistic originality, and led by natural transitions to the opera. Poetry was on the point of expiring; but music was rising to take her place' (*Renaissance in Italy*, 2 vols (London: Murray, 1921), II, 210).

[177] *Overture to the Opera*, pp. 86–87 (ll. 87–88); but see Tasso's 'rime selvagge' written by 'rozza mano in rozza scorza' at the end of the second chorus, pp. 149–50 (ll. 1175–80).

[178] Giovan M. Crescimbeni, *Dell'istoria della volgar poesia* and *Comentarj*, rev. 2nd edn, 6 vols (Venice: Basegio, 1730–31), I (1730), 383; on the 'stanze alla contadinesca', see ibid., p. 204. Cf. Giuseppe Maria Andrucci [Francesco S. Quadrio], *Della poesia italiana, libri due* (Venice: Zane, 1734), pp. 352–53.

[179] The 'earlier surviving "irregular" examples of drama', as pointed out by Lisa Sampson, already 'integrated pastoral and sometimes rustic subjects': see *Pastoral Drama in Early Modern Italy: The Making of a New Genre* (London: Legenda, 2006), p. 13. Cf. Daniel Javitch, 'The Emergence of Poetic Genre Theory in the Sixteenth Century', *Modern Language Quarterly*, 59 (1998), 139–69.

[180] See Isidoro Carini, *L'Arcadia dal 1690 al 1890*, 2 vols (Rome: Tipografia della Pace, 189), I: *Contributo alla storia letteraria d'Italia del secolo XVII e de' principii del XVIII*, 402–11.

selected by Dati and copied by the calligrapher Valerio Spada — a work which was later deemed immoral and burned after the poet's death.[181] In 1654 Christina abdicated her throne, converted to Catholicism and settled down in Rome, where she initiated a literary circle and sponsored, in particular, many musical works such as the first opera by Alessandro Scarlatti, a pastoral 'dramma per musica' entitled *Gli equivoci nel sembiante* (1679). The Academy of Arcadia was formally constituted after her death in 1690, and had a precise programmatic intent: 'esterminare il cattivo gusto' through the establishment of 'colonies' in the main Italian cities, as Crescimbeni pugnaciously claimed in his *Storia dell'Accademia degli Arcadi*.[182]

From the point of view of the Arcadian reaction, the poetic 'bad taste' was epitomized by Marino. The author of *Adone* (1623) exhausted Tasso's epic sentiment with his self-indulgent taste for conceits, but his influence was profound and extensive. Considering Malatesti's *Brindisi*, for instance, the toast of the Cyclops Durantino (*Colmami quella ciotola men labile*) was clearly written in imitation of the famous dithyrambic chorus in the seventh canto of the *Adone*, which contains three proparoxytone words in each line.[183] These verses were also included in the *Don Tarsia*,[184] a work that Malatesti thought would give him posthumous recognition:

> Questa è un'opera mia
> Per la quale ho speranza, e mi conforto,
> D'aver a vivere quando sarò morto

as he wrote in the *Dialogo* between the poet Astianatte Molino — one of his early pseudonyms — and the 'scapigliato' Galeazzo Titta.[185]

Unsurprisingly, a relevant model of *rima sdrucciola*, triple or 'slippery' rhyme, was Sannazaro's *Arcadia*, preferred by some madrigalists for its musical potential

---

[181] Cf. *Rime per la Regina di Svezia e per altri personaggi*, BR, MS Ricc. 3110.

[182] Giovan M. Crescimbeni, *Storia dell'Accademia degli Arcadi istituita in Roma l'anno 1690* (1712), ed. by Lariso Salaminio [Thomas J. Mathias] (London: Becket, 1804), p. 52. Cf. Maylender, I, 232–81. Tiraboschi also calls it the 'reo gusto' (VIII, 307). See Vernon Hyde Minor, *The Death of the Baroque and the Rhetoric of Good Taste* (Cambridge: Cambridge University Press, 2006).

[183] *Brindis*, p. 10. The 'brindisi' itself, according to Della Casa, was a form of foreignising bad taste: see Giovanni Della Casa, *Galatheo*, in *Rime et prose* (Venice: Bevilacqua, 1558), p. 165.

[184] The title name 'evokes the word "tarsia", a part of a wooden inlay, and likely derives from Galileo Galilei's criticism of Torquato Tasso's poetry', as Eva Struhal explained: 'the scientist compares Tasso's pompous language to wood inlays and criticizes that when closely observed they never create a coherent and convincing representation' ('Friendly Disagreements: Salvator Rosa and Lorenzo Lippi in Seventeenth-Century Florence', in *Salvator Rosa e il suo tempo (1615–1673)*, ed. by Sybille Ebert-Schifferer, Helen Langdon, and Caterina Volpi (Rome: Campisano, 2010), pp. 43–55 (pp. 44–46)).

[185] See *Dialogo di un Poeta e di uno Scapigliato: Astianatte Molino, Galeazzo Titta*, BNCF, MS Magl. VII. 392, fols 1–26; cf. BNCF, MS Magl. VII. 359, *Poesie diverse che ancora non sono alla stampa di diversi ed eccellentissimi Autori, messi insieme da Astianatte Molino l'anno 1645*: this

against the Petrarchan plain rhyme.[186] We could say that the late Renaissance drifted into the Baroque 'Canterellandovi | Con rime sdrucciole', as the eminent naturalist and Apatista Francesco Redi wrote in his celebrated *Bacco in Toscana* — which was a poetic guide to the wines of Tuscany in the form of a dithyrambic 'azione scenica'.[187]

Together with the anti-Marinesque reaction, the Arcadians led by Crescimbeni also fostered a return to the Petrarchan model, as codified by Pietro Bembo.[188] The Arcadian arrangement of 'erudizione' and 'buon gusto' can be epitomized by the 1711 edition of Petrarch's *Rime*, which is annotated (with some corrections) by the main creator of Italian mock-heroic poetry, Alessandro Tassoni.[189] This is also the spirit of the prefatory letter by the Crusca academicians to the *Poesie liriche toscane* (1817) by Thomas James Mathias, in which Milton's verse is positively characterized as 'opera d'un pastorello d'Arcadia che avesse voluto verseggiar petrarchesco'.[190]

The Florentine academies kept alive the cult of 'that sweet Tuskane Petrarke which did pearce | his Laura with love Sonnets'.[191] The Apatisti Academy, in particular, where Salvini says that the *buon gusto* was 'regola delle regole',[192]

---

notebook also contains several poems by Francini (including two dedicated to Galileo) and a copy of the anonymous *Il pianto d'Italia* (1617), which is attributed to Marino and not to the classicist poet Fulvio Testi, as generally believed (pp. 494–515, fols 207ʳ–17ᵛ); cf. Antonio Belloni, 'Testi, Tassoni o Marino?', in *Il Propugnatore: nuova serie*, 2/1 (1889), 454–66. Malatesti's *Dialogo* was transcribed by Neri as an appendix to his 1873 letter on Malatesti (pp. 103–8), together with other compositions, among which two tailed sonnets on Don Tarsia: in the first one, Don Tarsia clearly appears as a double of the poet (p. 109).

[186] See Leopold Silke, 'Madrigali sulle egloghe sdrucciole di Iacopo Sannazaro: struttura poetica e forma musicale', *Rivista italiana di musicologia*, 14 (1979), 102–27. Other notable examples can be found among the poems set to music in the first collection of *Scherzi musicali* (1607) by Claudio Monteverdi, like 'La pastorella' by Sannazaro, in *terza rima sdrucciola*, and 'Damigella' from Chiabrera's *Vendemmie* (p. 237–41), a dithyrambic *canzonetta* in plain rhyme.

[187] Francesco Redi, *Bacco in Toscana: ditirambo* (Florence: Matini, 1685), p. 20.

[188] 'After a profound study of the vernacular canon, Bembo decided', as Anthony Oldcorn explains, 'that the stylistic and thematic model for Italian verse was essentially Petrarch, the so-called father, paradoxically, of neo-Latin humanism' ('Bembo and the Classicist Tradition', in *CHIL*, pp. 252–68 (p. 253)).

[189] Ludovico A. Muratori, 'Dedicazione e Prefazione', in *Le rime di Francesco Petrarca: s'aggiungono le Considerazioni rivedute e ampliate d'Alessandro Tassoni, le Annotazioni di Girolamo Muzio, e le Osservazioni di L. A. Muratori* (Modena: Soliani, 1711), p. vii. On the controversy between Petrarchists and Marinists, see the *Comentario* by Pier Jacopo Martello, published with his *Canzoniere* (Rome: Gonzaga, 1710).

[190] Thomas J. Mathias, *Poesie liriche toscane* (Florence: Piatti, 1817), p. ix.

[191] Barnabe Barnes, *Parthenophil and Parthenophe* (1593), ed. by Victor A. Doyno (Carbondale: Southern Illinois University Press, 1971), p. 28.

[192] Anton M. Salvini, *Discorsi Accademici sopra alcuni dubbj proposti nell'Accademia degli Apatisti*, 3 vols (Venice: Pasinello, 1735), I, 289.

hosted regular lectures on Petrarch's *Triumphi*, but most of their papers were
dispersed or burned by a fire in the archive.[193] One of the very few surviving
Petrarchan lectures to the Apatisti was precisely by Malatesti, and it was delivered
in May 1637, namely in the same months when he put together the sonnets of *La
Tina* then dedicated to Milton.[194] Despite the rhetorical profession of being
'ignorantissimo', his lecture on four lines of the *Triumphus Cupidinis* (II. 184–
87) strived to be seriously erudite, but Arnaldo Della Torre comments that its
purple prose 'non ha in sé e per sé alcun pregio tale che valga a scusare chi l'ha
tolta dallo zibaldone'.[195] Such academic gravity was contrived, as it clearly appears
from a sonnet included in the same notebook, only a few pages before the lecture:

> Il Petrarca da Laura altro che inchini
> non ebbe, ché le donne anco in quei tempi
> non volevan sonetti ma quattrini.[196]

It is in this context that Malatesti's use of the Petrarchan sonnet, instead of the
octaves which were characteristic of both rustic poetry and burlesque *capitoli*,
represents a minor but noteworthy innovation.[197] It is not a unique attempt in

---

[193] See Lazzeri, p. 53: 'Di questa perdita il Gori fornisce come spiegazione sia la deprecabile
abitudine degli Apatisti reggenti di portare a casa propria i documenti in questione sia un
incendio avvenuto negli Archivi dell'Accademia'.

[194] BNCF, MS Magl. VII. 391, fols 156ʳ–76ʳ. This *coda* entitled *Malat[esti] Poesie* contains
almost all of the fifty rustic equivocations, with the exception of Sonnet XIV (see Valacca, p. 3),
all of them crossed out and therefore transcribed: the fair copy is arguably the one presented
to Milton.

[195] The literary critic, however, continues: 'Pregio invece ha se la si consideri come indice del
continuato culto del Petrarca nelle Accademie in Firenze e come mezzo di riannodamento tra
quel furore petrarchesco, diciamolo così, di cui furono prese nella seconda metà del
cinquecento le Accademie fiorentine, e quel fervido ritorno al Petrarca, di che si gloriarono
quelle stesse Accademie in sui primordi dell'Arcadia, che, com'è noto, credette di restaurare il
buon gusto e la semplicità della poesia promovendo il largo risveglio d'uno schietto
petrarchismo' (Arnaldo Della Torre, 'Una lezione di Antonio Malatesti su Petrarca
all'Accademia degli Apatisti', in *Padova in onore di Francesco Petrarca, MCMIV*, ed. by
Vincenzo Crescini, Francesco Flamini, Andrea Moschetti, and Albino Zenatti, 2 vols (Padua:
Società Cooperativa Tipografica, 1904–09), II: *Miscellanea di studi critici e ricerche erudite*
(1909), 59–74 (p. 61); Malatesti's lecture is here copied at pp. 74–83).

[196] BNCF, MS Magl. VII. 391, fol. 149ʳ. Another Apatista, Giovanni Battista C. Nelli, author
of an important *Saggio di storia letteraria fiorentina del secolo XVII* (Florence: Giuntini, 1759),
similarly commented on a Petrarchan sonnet to prove 'che Madonna Laura attaccasse un
pochino il Mal Franzese al Petrarca' (see BNCF, MS Magl. II. 33, fol. 47; cf. Benvenuti, p. 260).

[197] There are, of course, some other few but notable precedents to Malatesti's rustic sequence,
for example Del Bene's *Sonetto alla Tina da Campi che havea mandato un picchio e una pispola
a Meo* (in *Poesie varie*, BNCF, MS Magl. VII. 446, fol. 10ʳ). De Sanctis noted: 'The sonnet and
the *canzone* were looked upon as practically consecrated and unchangeable, and no one dared
to touch them profanely; therefore they remained as they were, without development. The new
spirit was making its way in the new form: in the *ottava rima* or the "stanza"' (I, 392). See also
Silvia Longhi, *Lusus: il capitolo burlesco nel Cinquecento* (Padova: Antenore, 1983), p. 4.

the genre, and Valacca pointed out that Allegri had just similarly replaced the rustic octaves with madrigals: it is possible, in fact, that 'lo spunto all'equivoco malatestiano sia stato preso dai madrigali equivoci della *Geva*' — and with mediocre results, according to the editor.[198] Like Julius Cerialis's *rura* in Martial's epigram, Malatesti's verses are certainly not 'aeterno proxima Vergilio' (XI. 52); but they are asserting a new style from within a lively Tuscan tradition and beyond the affected Petrarchism that we find, for instance, in Milton's Sonnet III, in which the poet compares his love to a 'pastorella' who cultivates foreign flowers in the Tuscan soil.[199]

Although the invention of *sonetti pastorali* is traditionally ascribed to the Florentine poet and historian Benedetto Varchi,[200] the rustic genre is not the same as the pastoral, while the later Arcadian attempts with the sonnet lacked of any *curiosa felicitas*. In the early seventeenth century we should mention, at least, Bracciolini's sonnets to *Lena fornaia*, a parody of Petrarch's *Canzoniere*.[201]

Beyond the academic jest, Malatesti's rustic sonnets should also be read in conjunction with the process of Tuscan domestication of the two-headed 'mostro di poesia' represented by the dithyramb, as Fioretti called — with ambiguous pride — his own *Polifemo briaco*, which clearly influenced the sonnets of the *Brindisi de' Ciclopi*.[202] The Carmelite scholar Teobaldo Ceva described this 'mostruous' genre as characterized by 'intollerabile gonfiezza di stile, ampollosità di sconcie e stravaganti figure, frequenza di parole composte oscure e pressoché incapaci di senso'.[203] In his introductory essay to *The Book of the Sonnet*, Leigh Hunt stated that the only unsuitable 'class of subjects' for the sonnet would be

---

[198] Valacca, p. 7.

[199] *Minor Poems*, pp. 50–51.

[200] Crescimbeni was sceptical: 'Se il Varchi sia stato inventore de' sonetti pastorali potrebbe porsi in dubbio, quantunque ciò venga affermato nella di lui vita impressa da' Giunti, poiché molti altri poeti ne scrissero nel tempo stesso, e fra gli altri Bernardo Tasso, che ne lasciò alcuno nel libro primo degli amori impresso nel 1532' (*Dell'istoria*, p. 280, n. 80).

[201] See Michele Barbi, *Notizia della vita e delle opere di Francesco Bracciolini* (Florence: Sansoni, 1897), pp. 85–86.

[202] The *Polifemo briaco* was published in the third volume of Fioretti's *Proginnasmi poetici* (Florence: Cecconcelli, 1627), pp. 549–50; in the enclosed *Documento per lo sopraddetto Ditirambo*, Fioretti wrote: 'Noi primi dunque senza special esempio né de' Greci, né de' Latini, dopo tanti secoli abbiamo in questa maschera mostruosa figurato questo mostro di poesia, con gran difficoltà dell'arte, rispetto alla nostra lingua, che non è atta né accomodevole a partorir simili mostruosità' (p. 551). It is significant that the author used the same definition for tragicomedy, with apparent negative connotations: 'Tragicommedia è un mostro di poesia tanto enorme e contraffatto, che i Centauri, gl'Ippogrifi, le Chimere appetto a questo sono parti graziosi, e perfetti' (ibid., p. 136).

[203] Teobaldo Ceva, *Dissertazione intorno a varj Lirici Componimenti*, in *Scelta di canzoni de' più eccellenti poeti antichi, e moderni*, ed. by Ignazio Gaione (Venice: Bassanese, 1756 ; 3rd edn Venice: Novelli, 1769), p. 75.

the dithyrambical, as it 'disdains all order and bounds'.[204] Even so, the double structure of the dithyramb, para-etymologically supported by the prefix 'di-', and its relative abundance of compound words match a key structural feature of the sonnet form. In fact, the sonnet had been exploited for a long time for its 'duplex structure', as Frank Templeton Prince emphasized in relation to Milton's use of pleonasm.[205]

The dithyrambic combination of duplicity and obscenity allowed a slippery progress, if not a renewal, of the Petrarchan form. The name of Berni's *capitoli* was taken from the division of the *Triumphi*, acknowledging the poetic code while developing it in new directions, and this is even more valid as regards the sonnet tradition, which very early became, as explained by Catherine Bates, a 'self-parodying genre'.[206] Malatesti's use of the sonnet, however, is not only and simply parodistic, but thoroughly equivocal.

Just as the sonnets addressed to Tina are not strophically tailed but maliciously 'scodati', as alluded in Sonnet XVIII (*Sopra lo scodar le galline*), they were neither composed according to the *equivoci rithimorum* that we may find in some of the earliest sonnets, based on the sporadic occurrence of rhyme words with equivocal meaning.[207] Through the newly found dithyrambic vein, grafted into Bernesque poetry and the comic-realistic 'nuovo trovato' of the Florentine Rustico di Filippo,[208] Malatesti's equivocations defiantly tackled and confronted the Petrarchan model in its content more than in its apparent form. His sonnets aim at what Jean Toscan called *équivoque globale*, in which the second level of reading, which carries the bawdy references, is developed to the point of blatancy.[209]

---

[204] *The Book of the Sonnet*, ed. by Leigh Hunt and Samuel Adams Lee, 2 vols (London: Sampson Low, Son & Marston, 1867), I, 5.
[205] Frank T. Prince, *The Italian Element in Milton's Verse* (Oxford: Clarendon Press, 1954), pp. 91–97. Dante Gabriel Rossetti epitomized the two-fold essence of the sonnet as follows: 'A Sonnet is a coin: its face reveals | The soul, — its converse, to what Power 'tis due' (*Ballads and Sonnets* (London: Ellis and White, 1881), p. 161).
[206] Catherine Bates, 'Desire, Discontent, Parody. The Love Sonnet in Early Modern England', in *The Cambridge Companion to the Sonnet*, ed. by Anthony D. Cousins and Peter Howarth (Cambridge: Cambridge University Press, 2011), pp. 105–24 (p. 120).
[207] Leandro Biadene, 'Morfologia del sonetto nei sec. XIII e XIV', *Studj di filologia romanza*, 4 (1889), 1–234 (pp. 154–56). The Paduan poet Antonio da Tempo already distinguished *equivocus simplex* and *equivocus compositus*: see *Delle rime volgari* (1332), ed. by Giusto Grion (Bologna: Romagnoli, 1869), pp. 160–62 (p. 160).
[208] See Mario Marti, 'La coscienza stilistica di Rustico di Filippo e la sua poesia', in *Cultura e stile nei poeti giocosi del tempo di Dante* (Pisa: Nistri-Lischi, 1953), pp. 41–58 (p. 46). Cf. Rustico Filippi, *Sonetti*, ed. by Pier V. Mengaldo (Turin: Einaudi, 1971); Joan H. Levin, *Rustico di Filippo and the Florentine Lyric Tradition* (New York: Lang, 1986).
[209] As a model of 'sporadic equivocation', in which the obscene level of reading is not always necessary, Toscan refers to Burchiello; as an example of 'global equivocation', he provides a translation of Lorenzo's 'canzone a ballo' entitled *Tra Empoli e Pontolmo* (CDL, IV, 1641–56). Antonio Belloni also explained that in Maltesti's sonnets 'l'equivoco deriva dal significato ambiguo a cui possono essere tratte, nel loro complesso, le immagini', as opposed to 'gli equivoci che poggiano sul doppio senso delle singole parole' (*Il Seicento* (Milan: Vallardi, 1947), p. 322).

Equivocations were typical of erotic poetry in the post-classicist phase of the Renaissance and represented, according to Antonio Marzo, 'una linea capace di portare la poesia fuori dalle secche degli schemi rigidamente petrarchisti'.[210] However, as argued by Danilo Romei, Toscan's idea of equivocal poetry as a 'langage à deux niveaux' needs further articulation, as we may find at least three main levels of interpretation: the literal level, which celebrates modest or ordinary subjects and derives from the classical tradition of the paradoxical encomium; a parodistic level, which can often be read as a double paradox built on the first level; and a level which is explicitly erotic and often associated with homosexual practices, mainly originating from the tradition of Carnival poetry which is, in turn, a parody of classical motives.[211] In its best results, this structure expands the vocabulary and creates a suggestive set of variations of an otherwise constrained imagery.

Considering that the *equivocatio* in the sonnet tradition was mainly used in a grammatical sense to denote semantic ambiguity in rhyming words, which Dante had already dismissed it as 'inutilis',[212] emphasis on gender ambiguity created a broader spectrum for the metaphorical possibilities of the equivocation. The gender shift from 'Nencia' to 'Nencio', for instance, is indicative of Malatesti's engagement with the genre; besides, as the anagram is a species of grammatical equivocation, we could also read *La Tina* as an anagrammatic feminine version of the poet's pseudonym 'Latoni'. The word 'sonetto' is itself affected by global equivocation: in burlesque poetry, in fact, the noun 'suono' and the verb 'suonare' were regularly used to connote sexual acts, while the diminutive suffix '-etto' marked the term in the semantic field of homosexual relationships.[213]

Malatesti's claim that his sonnets have a 'coda' should accordingly be taken as a declaration of style, with reference to the burlesque-realistic tradition of the tailed sonnet, but not only to this. In the proemial letter, Nencio says that he addressed his sonnets to his rustic muse as an expression of his love: 'Io non per altro ho diritto lo stile verso di te, che per mostrarti quanto io son cotto del tuo amore'. The word 'cotto' can be used figuratively as a synonym for 'avvinazzato', as noted in the first edition of the *Vocabolario degli Accademici della Crusca* (1612);[214]

---

[210] Antonio Marzo, *Note sulla poesia erotica del Cinquecento* (Lecce: Adriatica, 1999), p. 16.

[211] Danilo Romei, 'Il linguaggio dell'equivoco', in *Da Leone X a Clemente VII: scrittori toscani nella Roma dei papati medicei (1513–1534)* (Manziana: Vecchiarelli, 2007), pp. 243–66 (pp. 256–57). Carnival represents a general overturning of social orders, including the inversion of gender roles.

[212] See *De Vulgari Eloquentia*, II. xiii. 13. The rhyming word 'svelto' in Malatesti's Sonnet XXXI (*Sopra il susin torto*) is an example of grammatical equivocation.

[213] *CDL*, I. 1, 206 and 378. See e.g. Sonnet XIII, *Sopra il sonar lo zufolo*, not included in the 1650 MS dedicated to Cordini.

[214] *Vocabolario degli Accademici della Crusca* (Venice: Alberti, 1612; facsimile repr. Florence-Varese: Era, 2008), p. 235.

this concurs with the fact that these sonnets have a dithyrambic vein, as mentioned in the first quatrain of the first sonnet, *Sopra il sonetto con la coda*: 'cantando d'improviso alla carlona | sul suono, spinto dal calor del mosto'.[215] But the main obscene level of this address is built upon the use of the word 'stile' as a phallic metaphor, which underlies the ambiguity of the word 'diritto', meaning both 'addressed' and 'erect'.[216]

Sonnet II is precisely an equivocation *Sopra l'alzar lo stile*. In its parody of traditional love poetry, in particular, the rhyming qualification of Tina as 'gentile' infringes on the conventions of the Stilnovo. For Stilnovo poetry, as Jonathan Usher explains, 'it is love itself which initiates the literary act ("dittare" is the technical term for writing poetry), whereas the poet's function is to find appropriate verbal expression'.[217] For Malatesti, style fully incarnates passion rather than love, and in the dedicatory letter Nencio is appropriately described as an anti-Apatista: 'la passione è quella che mi muove il limbello in bocca'. His love sonnets, 'dettati' by 'una musa buffona', as stated in Sonnet I, are a literal instance of the famous dictum by the naturalist Comte De Buffon: 'Le style c'est l'homme même.'[218]

In summary, Malatesti's 'tailed' equivocations presume and leave behind the evolution of the tailed sonnet from the metrical to a fully metaphorical function. At the same time, the Petrarchan style is literalized for satirical effect. Annibal Caro, under the pseudonym 'Agresto da Ficaruolo', had already commented on the villanesque poem *Ficheide* (1539), by Francesco Maria Molza, in a way that signals with consummate irony the development of the new style: where Molza writes 'che tanto la mia penna onora', Agresto notes that 'Petrarca avrebbe detto, *che col mio stile incarno*'.[219] It was Caro who also invented the character

---

[215] As according to Toscan the verb 'cantare' was used as a synonym for 'paedicare' (*CDL*, I. 1, 361–62), while the verbs 'dire' (II, 1106–8) and 'vedere' (II, 1079–81) both denote 'agir par le sexe', we can follow the derivation of the adverbial expression 'all'improvviso' from 'all'in-pro-vista' (II, 1011) and read the line in which Lippi writes that Malatesti 'Canta improvviso' (*Malmantile*, p. 92, I. 61. 3) in connection with Berni's *Capitolo primo alla sua innamorata*: 'e dico all'improvista de' sonetti' (l. 32).

[216] Toscan further explains: '*Stile*, à travers l'acception de "stylet", est devenu un substitut métaphorique du "penis"' (*CDL*, II, 1151).

[217] Jonathan Usher, 'Origins and Duecento', in *CHIL*, pp. 3–36 (p. 27); cf. the ironic sonnet 'Mente ed umìle e più di mille sporte' by Onesto da Bologna, 'in which he pokes fun at the *stilnovisti* debating in a daze with hordes of hypostatic spirits, and spouting trendy buzzwords like "umile" with the stress indulgently moved *à la française* to the penultimate syllable (to rhyme with "gentile")' (ibid.).

[218] Georges-Louis Leclerc Comte de Buffon, *Discours sur le style* (1753), in *Histoire naturelle, générale et particulière. Supplément IV* (Paris: Imprimerie Royale, 1777), pp. 1–20. De Sanctis applied this *dictum* to the 'new literary criticism' of the eighteenth century (II, 924).

[219] Annibal Caro, *Commento di Ser Agresto da Ficaruolo sopra la prima ficata di padre Siceo* [Francesco M. Molza], *con la Diceria de' nasi* (Bologna: Romagnoli, [1584] 1861), p. 125. Gilbert suggests that 'Milton in his promiscuous reading probably had perused' this work (p. 59).

of Ser Fedocco, fictional author of a series of tailed sonnets called *Mattaccini*, to mock the commentator Lodovico Castelvetro, 'Edipo dei misteri di Petrarca',[220] and we find the proverbial Ser Fedocco towards the end of Nencio's letter. With his 'scodatura', Malatesti thus exposes the sonnet form to a parody of its epigonal practitioners, who did not develop a satirical style but paved the way for the 'effeminate' rhetoric of the Arcadian pastorals.[221] In this process, he brought together the burlesque and the rustic tradition of Tuscan poetry in a somewhat new genre, and first presented it in the form of a paradoxical encomium.

In a tailed sonnet prefaced to the *Stanze rusticali* by the Venetian nobleman Bartolomeo Vitturi, the Arcadian Gasparo Gozzi precisely defined the genre of rustic love poetry as a 'nuovo stil', inspired by 'Amor sazio d'udire *unquanco, e guari*'.[222] This line contains an intertextual reference to the founder of La Crusca and famous burlesque poet Anton Francesco Grazzini, known as 'il Lasca'. In his anthology of *Opere burlesche* (1548), Lasca addressed the reader with a parody of Petrarch's proemial sonnet *Voi ch'ascoltate in rime sparse il suono*, and praised Berni's 'stil senz'arte' because it did not offend the common ear with 'le lascivie del parlar Toscano', avoiding musty expressions such as 'unquanco' and 'guari'.[223] The 'lascivious' element of Tuscan language, it seems, was perceived not so much in concept, as in the ever imitative and most unimaginative use of Petrarch's style made by his epigones, and in particular by the rhetorical grammarians or 'pedanti'.

Vitturi's *Stanze rusticali* include a final octave by Marsili, which invites the reader who may not approve of this rustic new style to be quiet — 'poi pensi ciò che vuole in suo segreto'.[224] We can already find such a liberal and defiant attitude

---

[220] Annibal Caro, *Apologia degli Accademici dei Banchi di Roma contra Lodovico Castelvetro* (Parma: Viotto, 1558), now in *Opere*, ed. by Stefano Jacomuzzi (Turin: UTET, 1974), pp. 83–328 (p. 242); in a dreamlike conversation about style, Petrarch and Burchiello agree that Ser Fedocco's sonnets had to be 'con la coda!' (pp. 255–56). Cf. Agnolo di Cosimo (il Bronzino), *I salterelli all'Abbruccia sopra i mattacini di Ser Fedocco*, ed. by Carla Rossi Bellotto (Rome: Salerno Editrice, 1998).

[221] As noted by Gordon Braden, in the Renaissance the 'standard joke about the Petrarchan lover is his effeminacy' ('Gaspara Stampa and the Gender of Petrarchism', *Texas Studies in Literature and Language*, 38 (1996), 115–39 (p. 117). This also reinforces the preference of the Apatisti for the *Triumphi* over the *Canzoniere*: 'Non ci dice infatti il Nisieli che l'amore, che forma la sostanza del *Canzoniere*, fa condurre vita oziosa effeminata e volta a ignobilissimo scopo?' (Della Torre, p. 73).

[222] Bartolomeo Vitturi, *La serenata di Ciapino e Il lamento della Ghita: stanze rusticali* (Venice: Albrizzi, 1750), p. 2; cf. Gamba, p. 617. In 1750 Lami sent a copy of Vitturi's *Stanze* to Andrea Alamanni, as attested by a letter dated November 4 (BR, MS 3699, fol. 258). In Malatesti's Sonnet XXIII, *Sopra le pesche*, Ciapin is mentioned as Tina's brother.

[223] See 'Il Lasca a chi legge', in *Il primo libro dell'opere burlesche di M. Francesco Berni, di M. Gio. Della Casa, del Varchi, del Mauro, del Bino, del Molza, del Dolce, e del Firenzuola* [Florence: Giunti, 1548], ed. by P. Antinoo Rullo [Paolo Antonio Rolli] with notes by Antinoo Nivalsi [A. M. Salvini] (London: Pickard, 1721), p. xxii; Lasca proclaimed Berni as 'vero trovatore, | maestro e padre del burlesco stile' (p. xxi).

[224] In 1747 Gasparo and his brother Carlo Gozzi founded a Venetian academy of Bernesque poets called 'Granellesca', which had a particular interest in Tuscan rustic poetry and included

in the opening address of the aforementioned *Rime piacevoli*, dated January 1642 (1643), in which Coltellini declares that his equivocal 'scherzi poetici' could only be frowned upon by straitlaced pedants, and advises them to keep away from any book which bears a title like 'Rime piacevoli, o burlesche, o alla bernesca'.[225] Coltellini's arguments in support of equivocal poetry are even more remarkable considering that he was a censor of the Holy Office. On a general level, according to Benvenuti, he defended poetic freedom against those readers who appeared to be scandalized 'se la povera musa burlesca fra gli stracci della sua veste lasciava ancora vedere un po' di ciccia provocante'.[226] This was also the sense of his *Endecasyllabi fidentiani* (1641), which lampooned the pedants with a particular irony against the pederastic care for the education of their young pupils.[227] The model of this sub-genre of burlesque poetry was the Vicentine jurist Camillo Scroffa (*c.* 1525–1564), known as 'Fidenzio Glottocriso Ludimagistro', who also opened his *Cantici* (1562) with the parodistic sonnet *Voi ch'auribus arrectis auscultate*, and Oldcorn effectively commented: 'Petrarch's liminal sonnet, a sacred cow if ever there was one, imitated with a straight face by every rhymester in Europe, is made new by the fresh content and context'.[228]

The contention against pedantry demands originality, and this is quite relevant to understanding Malatesti's poetic stance and the general poetics of his century. When Lasca writes that Varchi cultivated the Parnassus 'insegnando a' pedanti il parlar Tosco', for instance, he is also taunting his essential Petrarchan 'effeminacy', as becomes clear from the first lines, where he states that Bembo was awaiting Varchi in the Elysian Fields 'a braccia aperte e brache calate'.[229] The

among its members Marsili and Baretti: see Carlo Gozzi, *Memorie inutili* (1797), ed. by Paolo Bosisio and Valentina Garavaglia, 2 vols (Milan: LED, 2006), I, 363–74. In the *Frusta letteraria* of 1 April 1764, Baretti praised Marsili's style, but omitted his name (*Opere*, II (1813), 118).

[225] *Rime piacevoli*, p. 11. On the cover, Coltellini put the following epigraph from Martial: 'Absit a iocorum nostrum simplicitate malignus interpres'.

[226] Benvenuti, p. 150.

[227] In 1652 Coltellini also published the second part of his *Endecasyllabi fidentiani*, which included a section with the self-explanatory title *Gyneroticomania seu Muliebramorose-deliramento di Ser Poi Iuniore*, dedicated to Chimentelli, and a *Dialogo Rhytmico, seu Sonetto Etrusco tra 'l Discipulo e 'l Pedagogo*, dedicated 'All'ingegnoso Signore Antonio Malatesti, Poeta Lepidissimo, Epico, Lirico, Enigmatico, Faceto, &c.' (*Endecasyllabi Fidentiani del signor Ostilio Contalgeni Accademico Apatista: parte seconda* (Florence: Massi, 1652), pp. 16–22, 26–27). The first part of Coltellini's *Endecasyllabi* (Florence: Tipografia Massi Landiana, 1641) already contained many obscene equivocations, like the following *excusatio* for the addition of the burlesque-pastoral poems *La Fistula del magistro Ficardo*, probably by Fioretti: 'le collocai dietro a' miei Endecasillabi, non perché io non conoscessi, che per più cagioni dovevano star innanzi, ma per non mostrare di voler prima donare le cose altrui che le mie, e per altri degni rispetti. Ricevete dunque cortesi Lettori questa Fistula dove io ve la metto, senza pensar ad altro, e vivete felici' (p. 81). See Arturo Graf, 'I pedanti', in *Attraverso il Cinquecento* (Turin: Loescher, 1888), pp. 171–213.

[228] 'The Anti-Classicist Tradition', p. 275.

[229] Anton F. Grazzini, *Opere*, ed. by Guido Davico-Bonino (Turin: UTET, 1974), pp. 300–01.

argument against derivative Petrarchism is almost logically embedded in burlesque poetry: this genre was praised by Varchi for its 'naturalità e fiorentinità',[230] and the practice of sodomy was reputed so 'natural and Florentine' that it was also known as *vizio fiorentino*.[231]

To be sure, there was a classical tradition that validated (male) homoerotic practices as a natural privilege of the cultivated nobility and clergy. Ernst Curtius refers to an 'anonymous metrical debate' of the twelfth century, for example, where the love of boys is defined as a divine *ludus*, while the 'rustici' are described like animals that 'cum mulieribus debent inquinari'.[232] Accordingly, as Toscan explains, rustic poetry was concerned with the 'usurpation paysanne', and in particular it poked fun at the peasants' pretence to be as refined as the aristocracy in their erotic activity,[233] rather than just *pecudes* for production and reproduction — 'per solo desio d'aver figliuoli', as Gozzi defined the mainspring of the *Stanze rusticali*.

Because of the shifting social and cultural conditions of this classical topos, pedants are now ridiculed as much as peasants, and the question of style becomes essential to the legitimation of rustic poetry beyond the burlesque genre. As the main distinctive trait of a gentleman lies in his 'stile fino', in the dedicatory letter of *La Tina* Nencio incites his rustic muse to refine his style: 'se lo stile a prima vista ti pare grosso, con la tua efficacia compisci il suo difetto'. Another example is the collection of *Strambotti alla villanesca* by the notorious satirist and polygraph Pietro Aretino, which was accompanied by the previous *Stanze de la Serena* (1537) with the overt purpose of a 'comparatione degli stili' — and in a prefatory letter he also announces a new *Nencia*, which will be soon 'drizzata' to one of his courtly friends.[234]

---

[230] Benedetto Varchi, *L'Hercolano* (1570), ed. by Antonio Sorella, 2 vols (Pescara: Libreria dell'Università Editrice, 1995), II, 806. Cf. Varchi's *Lezione della poetica in generale* (1553), in *Opere*, 2 vols (Trieste : Racheli, 1859), II, 681–93: 'Ed io porto ferma opinione, che chi non è nato a Firenze, o almeno stato in Firenze assai, non possa in questo genere devenire eccellente' (p. 691). Toscan also comments: 'Si l'on pose l'hypothèse que certains *capitoli* de Berni déroulent un double discours, on est fondé de penser que le deuxième est de convention, mais qu'à l'instar du premier, il est d'essence florentine' (*CDL*, I. 1, 21–22).

[231] In 1305 the Domincan preacher Giordano of Pisa claimed that Florence was a new 'Soddoma': see *Prediche inedite, recitate in Firenze dal 1305 al 1305*, ed. by Enrico Narducci (Bologna: Romagnoli, 1867), p. 449. Cf. Michael Rocke, *Forbidden Friendships: Homosexuality and Male Culture in Renaissance Florence* (Oxford: Oxford University Press, 1998).

[232] Ernst R. Curtius, *Europäische Literatur und lateinisches Mittelalter* (1948), trans. by Williard R. Trask and Peter Godman, *European Literature and Latin Middle Ages*, 7th edn (Princeton: Princeton University Press, 1990), pp. 116–17; cf. *CDL*, I. 1, 199.

[233] *CDL*, I. 1, 201–04. For the satire against the peasants, one need only recall the octaves of the *Sferza de' Villani*, which begins with a parody of Petrarch's Sonnet II, 'Per fare una leggiadra sua vendetta': see Domenico Merlini, *Saggio di ricerche sulla satira contro il villano* (Milan: Loescher, 1894).

[234] Pietro Aretino, *Strambotti a la Villanesca, freniticati da la quartana de l'Aretino: con le Stanze de la Serena appresso in comparatione degli stili* (Venice: Marcolini, 1544). De Sanctis

In this context, it is fair to say that *La Tina* was not simply 'the poem of the city caricaturing the village', as it was *La Nencia* according to De Sanctis but neither is it true that in Malatesti's hendecasyllables 'we smell the village', as in *La Beca*.[235] The caricature is fraught with coarse vulgarity, and yet the *volgare* strives for natural and Florentine expression. More than 'irridente umanità del signore pel villano', the new rustic style pursues an essential interest in popular language, an intellectual passion for the metaphorical qualities of the 'proverb' (*pro verbo*), as Arnaldo Alterocca explained for Lippi's *Malmantile*, and the 'proverbi del contado' in particular.[236]

In the *Dialogo di un Poeta*, Malatesti admits that

> La Tina da Castello
> Non piace perch'ella ha troppi bei detti
> Non ha da Contadina anco i concetti.[237]

Commenting on this poetic self-assessment, Valacca concluded that the literary value of Malatesti's *equivoci* would be better judged from the viewpoint of their relation to the *enimmi*: 'Questi infatti a primo aspetto dànno un senso osceno, mentre il senso riposto è innocente; quelli al contrario hanno il senso letterale innocente, mentre, diciam così, l'allegoria è spesso turpemente oscena'.[238] It would be an oversimplification to assume that the respective genres remain unaffected by this symmetry. The fact that Malatesti composed his equivocations together with the enigmatic sonnets can be confirmed by the 1637 dedicatory letter *Nencio alla Tina*, which is contained in the same manuscript notebook of *La Sfinge*.[239] Their obscene content, on the other hand, is not simply derivative of burlesque rusticity. As noted by De Fillippis, obscenity is 'one of the most pronounced characteristics of Italian riddles'.[240] Among others, the Sienese Angelo Cenni is a good example of both enigmatic (and mostly tailed) sonnets and rustic 'stanze alla martorella', published on behalf of the Academy of the Rozzi, which were 'famous for the impetus they gave to the development of the popular or rustic drama in the sixteenth century'.[241]

---

noted: 'Never was the saying that "the style is the man" so proved as in Aretino' (II, 613), and related to this style a 'period to his lover' by Giordano Bruno, where the lover is called 'tiller of the field of my soul' (p. 720; but the equivocal expression 'assottigliatogli il stile' is translated as 'softened the soil').

[235] De Sanctis, I, 395–96.

[236] Alterocca, pp. 104–05.

[237] BNCF, MS Magl. VII. 392, fol. 7^v; see Neri, p. 106.

[238] Valacca, p. 6.

[239] BNCF, MS Magl. VII. 674, fols 138^r–141^r.

[240] De Filippis, I, 1, 13. Demetrio Tolosani and Alberto Rastrelli remarked that most of Malatesti's unpublished riddles and many of those which were published with the censor's licence are quite 'evidenti' in their obscene meaning: *Enimmistica*, 2 vols (Milan: Hoepli, 1926; 3rd edn 1938), I, 26.

[241] De Filippis, I, 8.

Despite some arguable evidence that Malatesti's rustic equivocations are 'anything but stupid, and far from being enigmatic, they are comically clear', as John Arthos dismissively put it,[242] their main interest resides in the position that they carve out in the history of the sonnet through the contamination of riddles and burlesque equivocations within the genre of rustic poetry. Malatesti tries to open up the genre through global equivocation, which enhances the logical exhaustion of the sonnet's metaphorical conventions in both the classicist and the anti-classicist poetics.[243]

In fact, there is a logical argument that Coltellini puts forward in defence of his poetic 'equivoci & anfibologie', and this is that they could not reasonably bear any immoral consequence for the honest reader: 'E come potrebbe mai apprendere il concetto, chi non sa il proprio significato delle parole?'[244] An equivocal middle term, according to Aristotle, only produces fallacious deductions; on the other hand, as Coltellini further argues, Boccaccio would hold that a reduction of 'equivoci' to 'univoci' would make poetry impossible. This logical argument is strictly related to the theory of metaphor, which emphasizes the new theoretical approach to poetic forms, and in particular to the 'almost syllogistic' structure of the sonnet[245] — an intellectual vein that runs through the early modern poetics of witty concepts.

Tasso's *Discorsi del poema eroico* (1594) may offer a starting point. In the second book, Tasso explains that the 'equivoco' is a form of poetic sophism which 'prende gli auditori del suo piacere' and is particularly 'usato da' poeti toscani ne l'amorose poesie'.[246] The case for 'poesia piacevole' is made in the fourth book, where we find a distinction between metaphors devised for linguistic need, like those of the 'villani', and metaphors created for delight and ornament of diction: according to Aristotle, a proper metaphor is only of this second kind, which gives 'diletto oltre la necessità', while rustic metaphors are more precisely 'nomi equivoci'.[247]

---

[242] Arthos, p. 27.

[243] See Paola Cisternino, 'Aspetti della poesia burlesca del Seicento: gli *Enimmi* di Antonio Malatesti', in *I Capricci di Proteo*, pp. 773–81. See also Antonio Marzo, 'La lingua come distintivo di genere: il caso della letteratura erotica del Cinquecento', in *Atti del Terzo Convegno della Società Italiana di Linguistica e Filologia Italiana* (Napoli: ESI, 1997), pp. 417–30.

[244] *Rime piacevoli*, p. 10. Cf. Arthos, pp. 25–26. A similar argument is endorsed by Milton, in particular in his 1655 *Defensio* against More, as explained by Gilbert: 'Milton holds that an obscene subject may properly be dealt with in obscene terms by the most honorable and modest men' (p. 63).

[245] See Usher, 'Origins and Duecento', p. 12.

[246] Torquato Tasso, *Discorsi del poema eroico* (Naples: Stigliola, 1594), p. 28; see *Discourses on the Heroic Poem*, trans. by Mariella Cavalchini and Irene Samuel (Oxford: Clarendon Press, 1973).

[247] *Discorsi*, pp. 115–16. As an example of such equivocations, we can mention Tasso's own poem 'Signor Mosto, il vostro orto è così grande': see *Le rime*, ed. by Bruno Basile (Rome: Salerno Editrice, 1994), p. 846.

A systematic analysis can be found in the *Cannocchiale aristotelico* (1670), by Emanuele Tesauro. The Jesuit rhetorician refers the equivocation to the third species of metaphor discussed by Aristotle. In its simplest form, the 'metafora di equivoco' consists in the use of the same word with a different meaning. After a profusion of examples on the conceptual and grammatical levels which may be affected by semantic change, Tesauro concludes his exposition with what he calls 'l'Intenzion della mente': from equivocal intentionality, he suggests, 'nascono Enigmi talmente ambigui, che Iddio solo è quegli che può guardarcene'.[248]

We glimpse here an unprecedented articulation of the dramatic potential of the *equivoci* through the rhetorical subsumption of the *enimmi*. It is with a better understanding of the 'metaphor of equivocation' between Tasso and Tesauro, in conclusion, that we may reconsider *La Tina*'s ingenious sonnets in the rustic genre, and Malatesti's place in the history of seventeenth-century Italian poetry.

---

[248] Emanuele Tesauro, 'Metafora terza: di equivoco', in *Il Cannocchiale Aristotelico: o sia Idea dell'Arguta et Ingeniosa Elocutione che serve a tutta l'Arte Oratoria, Lapidaria, et Simbolica, Esaminata co' Principij del Divino Aristotele* (Turin: Zavatta, 1670), pp. 365–96 (p. 387).

LA
Tina Equiuoci Rusticali
di Antonio Malatesti cō
posti nella sua Villa di
Taiano il Settembre dell'
L'Anno 1637.

Sonetti Cinquãta.
Dedicati all' Ill.mo Signore
Et Padrone Oss.mo IL Signor'
Giouanni Milton Nobil'
Inghilese ~

NOTIZIE INTORNO ALL'AUTORE
Giuseppe Baretti[1]

~

Antonio Malatesti cittadino fiorentino discese da un'antica e riguardevole famiglia distinta in prima dal cognome de' Griffoli, oriunda da Terranuova, castello nel territorio d'Arezzo.

Suo padre fu Emilio figliuolo di Antonio di Malatesta di Ser Giovambattista di Messer Antonio Griffoli, il qual cognome fu mutato in quello di Malatesti mediante il suddetto Malatesta di Ser Giovambattista; e nella persona di esso Giovambattista di questa famiglia ammessa alla cittadinanza fiorentina l'anno 1531.

Nella Chiesa di Santa Croce di Firenze presso il pilastro del pulpito si vede la sepoltura de' Malatesti, ove giace il nostro Antonio, consistente in una lastrona di marmo intagliato coll'arme, che è un campo diviso per lo lungo, da una parte rosso con un grifo nero di cinghiale dentro, a cui allude il doppio cognome che ha avuto questa famiglia, e dall'altra parte è una banda per lo piano composta di scacchi neri e d'oro in campo bianco, e aveva già questa iscrizione:

> *Antonio Griffolo Jur. Consulto de Terranova Joannes Baptista Fil. Patri de se*
> *opt. merito, et sibi posterisque suis posuit anno 1503. Die 2 Mensis Januarij.*

Dalla civiltà tramandatagli da' suoi antenati non tralignò già il nostro Antonio, il quale benchè la fortuna o l'altrui consiglio lo facesse al negozio della seta applicare,[2] cominciò giovanetto a frequentare la celebre accademia degli Apatisti poco dopo il principio di essa, e col letteratissimo Agostino Coltellini dell'Accademia fondatore con nodo di virtuosa amicizia si strinse; e perché costume era di que' tempi che gli accademici il nome si mutavano, egli converse il suo nello anagrammatico di Alamonio Tansetti, che poi iscambiò in quello di Aminta Setajolo.

---

[1] As outlined in the *Introduction*, section 3, Baretti's two main intertexts are: Domenico Maria Manni, 'Prefazione', in *Brindisi d'Antonio Malatesti e di Pietro Salvetti* (Florence: Manni, 1723), pp. xi–xxviiii; and Giovanni Lami, *Notizia intorno all'autore*, in Antonio Malatesti, *La Tina* (London [Venice]: Edlin [Alvisopoli], 1757 [ca. 1837]), pp. 7–12; both texts are based on Francesco Cionacci, *Notizie del Sig. Antonio Malatesti*, BNCF, MS Magl. IX. 50 (n. 34), fols 134^{r-v} and 143^r. Relevant differences between Baretti's text and his sources are here reported in footnotes.

[2] '[...] per lo quale la Città di Firenze si è sempre in ogni secolo molto distinta; nondimeno il suo pronto, e spiritoso ingegno, animandolo, e spronandolo il suo buon genio, prese con forte desio ad amare il chiarissimo splendore della Fama, *Che trae l'Uom dal sepolcro, e in vita il serba*; e perciò cominciò a frequentare' etc. (Manni, p. xviiii).

In quest'Accademia il Malatesti[3] moltissime sue poetiche composizioni recitò, e spezialmente i suoi vaghissimi sonetti enimmatici, parte de' quali fu poi data alle stampe in Firenze nel 1723.[4]

Egli godè l'amicizia e la stima di tutti i letterati fiorentini del suo tempo; e particolarmente, oltre al nominato Coltellini, quella del gran Galileo, di Valerio Chimentelli, di Carlo Dati, di Francesco Redi, e d'Antonio Magliabecchi; e molto famigliarmente visse con Lorenzo Lippi buon pittore e valoroso poeta, quello di cui sotto nome di Perlone Zipoli abbiamo il giocondo poema del Malmantile, nel quale poema il nostro Antonio è mentovato sotto nome anagrammatico di Amostante Latoni, e il suo carattere è costì ritratto con propria e piacevole espressione.[5]

Benché il Malatesti fosse molto tirato al comporre poeticamente, pure rivolse anco l'ingegno a studi creduti dal mondo più gravi e più difficili. Già fatto uomo prese a studiare l'astronomia sotto la direzione del Dottore Lodovico Serenai, amicissimo del gran filosofo e mattematico Evangelista Torricelli, e non mal profitto vi fece; mostrò anzi che se nell'adolescenza allo studio delle scienze si fosse dato, dottissimo uomo divenuto sarebbe. Egli è ben vero che la inclinazione sua più forte e più naturale era quella verso la poesia; e tanto amore e sì intenso a quella portò, che non solo in tutto il corso non breve di sua vita egli continuamente compose; ma altresì con efficace attenzione e diligenza andò copiando quante poesie volgari e d'ogni genere non ancora stampate potè raccogliere, talché un bel numero di libri e zibaldoni ne venne a formare; da' quali poi Carlo Dati scelse la maggior parte di quelle da esso stimate migliori, e fattele da Valerio Spada Colligiano eccellente chirografo ricopiare, furono in più tomi mandate l'anno 1652 nella Svezia alla Regina Cristina dal Principe Leopoldo di Toscana che fu poi Cardinale. Gli zibaldoni del Malatesti furono dopo la sua morte gettati nelle fiamme, perché molte composizioni contra i buoni costumi contenevano.

Non solo il Malatesti riusciva degno di lode nelle opere che al tavolino lavorava, ma e' si fece anche conoscere per molto vivace e leggiadro nello improvvisare, per la qual cosa, oltre all'universale applauso, si meritò la grazia ed il favore de'

---

[3] '[...] in mezzo ad un buon numero di *Compagni d'alto ingegno*, moltissime' etc. (Manni, p. xviiii).

[4] Baretti clearly refers to Manni's edition of the *Brindisi*, not to the *Enimmi*, 'co' quali, non solamente risvegliò altri alla sua imitazione, ma gloria singolare acquistossi altresì, la quale poi molto gli s'accrebbe, quando buona parte di quelli fu data alle stampe' (Manni, pp. xix–xx).

[5] '[...] e il suo carattere vi è ritratto con la seguente propria e piacevol pittura, alludendo ancora all'essere egli stato di corpo adusto e gambe sottili: *È general di tutta questa mandra | Amostante Laton poeta insigne; | Canta improvviso come una calandra, | Stampa gli Enigmi, strologa e dipigne; | Lasciò gran tempo fa le polpe in Fiandra | Mentre si dava il Gallo a certe vigne; | Fortuna, che l'avea matto provato, | Volle ch'e' diventasse anche spolpato*' (Lami, p. 9). The phrase 'piacevole espressione' is taken from Manni's edition (p. xx), followed by Baretti, where the quotation from Lippi's *Malmantile* occurs at a later point (see below).

Principi Lorenzo e Mattias di Toscana, i quali essendosi di lui frequentemente serviti per comporre ottave, canzoni, e cartelli in occasione di mascherate, di calci, e di giostre, ne fecero rimunerare dal Gran Duca Ferdinando Secondo con un impiego nell'offizio del sale; e allora fu che egli abbandonò il negozio della seta, attendendo diligentemente a questo sino alla morte, che accadde l'anno 1672 il dì 27 di Dicembre.[6]

Compose il Malatesti i graziosi Brindisi de' Ciclopi, un grandissimo numero di sonetti enimmatici, il Don Tarsia, la Bita, il Capitano Comico, la Bella Spiritata, le poesie liriche, le poesie sacre, e un buon numero di capitoli, e altre cose, sì gravi come giocose, onde ben si può dire ch'egli entra in compagnia di coloro *che a ben far' poser' gl'ingegni*.[7]

Di lui fecero onorata menzione Paolo Minucci nelle note al Malmantile, il Coltellini nelle sue opere, Giovanmario Crescimbeni in più luoghi de' suoi Commentari all'Istoria della volgar poesia, e il Gesuita Giulio Negri nell'Istoria degli scrittori fiorentini.

Di questa *Tina* non si aveva notizia. Forse l'autore regalò questa copia scritta di sua mano al celeberrimo inglese nominato nel frontispizio.[8]

---

[6] 'E per interamente rappresentare più al vivo, che si puote, il nostro Poeta, tralasciare non si vuole che egli fu di lieto ed allegro umore, pronto e vivace nelle risposte, e di gioconda ed aggradevole conversazione; di maniera che il suo amico Lorenzo Lippi nel fece nel *Malmantile* questa piacevole pittura, alludendo ancora' etc. as in Lami's text, but with the correct quotation from Lippi 'si dava il Sacco' instead of 'si dava il Gallo' (Manni, pp. xxii–xxiii); Manni's text continues: 'Tralle Lettere di Francesco Redi stampate in Padova, e che ora si ristampano, insieme con molte altre, in Firenze da Giuseppe Manni, n'ha una indirizzata a Carlo Dati, nella quale così si parla del Malatesti. *Il Sig. Conte Ferdinando del Maestro fu iersera a veglia meco, e di più a cena, e cenammo testa a testa, e bevemmo alla salute di V.S. Illustriss. il vino rosso di Pietra Nera, che mi dona il Serenissimo Granduca. Quel che fu il bello si è che a mezza cena comparve il Sig. Antonio Malatesti, ed il buon uomo volle mettersi a tavola , e bevve più che la sua parte di quel Pietra Nera, innacquandolo per ischerzo con certo Trebbiano di Spagna delle Vigne di Castello. Basta, lo rimandai a casa in carrozza, ed il Sig. Conte Ferdinando ve lo accompagnò. Stamattina è ritornato a casa mia, che non era ancora levato , e voleva far la zuppa in quel Trebbiano, e mi ha portata la copia di sei nuovi Enigmi che ha fatti, che veramente son belli, ma belli davvero. Ne manderò a V. S. Illustriss. una copia, quando il suo servitore ritornerà costi quest'altra volta.* Dal paragrafo di questa lettera ben si conosce non solo l'allegra e sollazzevole conversazione di lui, ma ancora quanta stima ne facesse quel gran filosofo e poeta, a cui era ben noto, oltre al buon gusto e discernimento di Antonio, quanto ancora composto avea: poiché, siccome si ricava dalle *Selve MSS. per li Comentarj dell'Accademia degli Apatisti*, distese già da Francesco Cionacci, e somministratemi dalla gentilezza dell'eruditissimo Salvino Salvini Canonico Fiorentino, dalle quali ho preso non poche delle suddette notizie, e come si ricava ancora da altre memorie, egli compose, oltre a i presenti Brindisi, i quali di maggior numero dovrebbero essere, ma se n'è smarrito il restante, egli compose, dico, un grandissimo numero di Sonetti Enimmatici' etc. (pp. xxiii–xxv).

[7] Dante, *Inferno*, VI. 81.

[8] 'De' suoi Sonetti di equivoci rusticali intitolati la *Tina* non si aveva notizia. Egli dee averne regalata una copia scritta di sua mano al celeberrimo inglese nominato nel frontespizio, e da quella copia appunto la presente fedelmente è tratta' (Lami, p. 12).

La Tina
Equivoci rusticali
di Antonio Malatesti
composti nella sua Villa
di Taiano il settembre
dell'anno 1637

Sonetti cinquanta
dedicati all'Ill.mo Signore
et Padrone Oss.mo il Signor
Giovanni Milton
Nobil'Inghilese

NENCIO ALLA TINA

Non ti maravigliare, o Tina, se io nato tra le zolle, e più avvezzo a maneggiar la vanga ch'a impiastricciar i fogli, mi son lasciato imbecherare[1] da certi perdigiorni, che fanno quassù in contado dar le mosse ai tremuoti,[2] a compor versi a mazzastanga,[3] perché l'aria qui d'intorno a Firenze lo dà.[4] Non vedi tu che per tutto dove l'uom sia, alza una lastra e salta su un poeta? Io non per altro ho diritto lo stile verso di te, che per mostrarti quanto io son cotto del tuo amore. Sappi che tutta la notte mi sto colla penna in mano stropicciando la vena al mio cervello, stillando l'ingegno a gocciole su queste tantafere:[5] accettale cortesemente, o Tina, e se lo stile a prima vista ti par grosso, con la tua efficacia compisci il suo difetto, perché io scrivendo a vanvera ho fatto d'ogni erba un fascio, e sono andato menando così il can per l'aia[6] per isfogare la rabbia che mi manuca[7] per il martello ch'i' ho de' fatti tuoi; e se ti pare ch'i' abbia preso vento,[8] cioè che nel più bello del lagoro[9] io sia arrenato, tu sai che chi fa falla,[10] e gli[11] erra, come dice il proverbio, il prete all'altare. Non ci posso far altro s'io ti do tutto quel poco di talento ch'io mi trovo, non mi pare che tu ti debba dolere: conosco bene che la tua crudeltà è tanto grande, e la mia cattiva fortuna è tale ch'io non posso toccare il fondamento della causa del mio penare, né commuoverti a compassione di me. Anzi, quanto più vo[12] grattando il corpo alla cicala,[13] più tu fai formicon di sorbo[14] e te ne stai soda al macchione,[15] ponendo, mentr'io favello, una vigna,[16] e lasciandomi predicare ai porri;[17] e so molto bene

---

[1] To be led on, possibly denominal from *bicchiere*, with ref. to the phrase *dare il vino*, to talk into.

[2] 'Make earthquakes', claim unbounded authority.

[3] 'With a sledge hammer', energetically.

[4] Inspires it.

[5] Trivial and long-winded compositions, possibly from *tanta fera*, an oversized animal mask used for Carnival.

[6] 'I have gone round and round', beaten about the bush.

[7] Is eating me, from Lat. *manducare*.

[8] 'Made a boast', lit. taken wind.

[9] Tuscan alteration of *lavoro*.

[10] *Chi fa falla, e chi non fa sfarfalla*, lit. anyone who does, does wrong; who does not, does err.

[11] Truncated form of third pers. m. pronoun *egli*, also commonly used as impers. or pl. subject; the alternative truncated form *e'* and the syncopate *ei* are generally preferred before consonant.

[12] Tuscan pop. sync. of *vado*, here used as auxiliary to expresses the present continuous.

[13] 'The harder I try to sing', lit. scratch the belly of the cicada.

[14] 'You remain indifferent to the provocation', lit. like an ant in a crab tree.

[15] 'Stand still in the briars.'

[16] 'Paying no attention', lit. planting a vineyard.

[17] Waste my breath, lit. preach to the leeks.

che queste mie caccabaldole[18] ti danno piuttosto ricadia[19] che alleggiamento, e che tutto questo avviene perché tu hai paglia in becco.[20] Scasimodeo![21] tu hai trovo[22] qualcuno di questi foramelli[23] che fanno il Ser Saccente, o il Tuttosalle, che ti gaveggia[24] di soppiatto. Ma se il diascolo[25] fa che io me n'addìa[26] e che io metta fuoco alla bombarda, ti mostrerò ch'io son buono per farla a te e a lui: in fe' di dieci,[27] senza stare a dirgli che vadia alle birbe[28] e badi ai fatti suoi, gli canterò una zolfa[29] che gli parrà forse più infruscata che non è il vespro degli Ermini,[30] perché tu sai che a me non mancano i modi per far delle bischenche[31] a uno quando i' voglio; e non gli gioverà l'andare con il calzar del piombo,[32] tanto andrà il mucino al lardo ch'e' vi lascerà la zampa,[33] e conoscerà poi ch'e' gli sta il dovere, e vedrà quel che gl'interviene a chi rompe l'uova in bocca alla brigata;[34] benché io faccia la gatta di Masino,[35] o per dir meglio il Ser Fedocco,[36] Tina, i' conosco il pel nell'uovo,[37] perché ho pisciato in più d'una neve,[38] e quando il tuo diavol nacque il mio andava alla panca.[39] Scusami s'io parlo troppo: la passione è quella che mi muove il limbello[40] in bocca. Io non posso sentire tutto il giorno qui in vicinanza tanti cicalecci[41] che legghino sempre in sul mio libro, perché mi par d'essere diventato lo spazzaforno[42] di questo paese. Altro non ho da dirti; leggi queste poesie ch'io ti mando non per pascerti di parole, ma per mostrarti la via del venire ai fatti. Sta sana, e voglimi bene sì com'io voglio a te.

[18] 'Blandishments', possibly popular alteration of *cabala*.
[19] Nuisance, from *ricadere*.
[20] 'You have something up your sleeve.'
[21] Good grief! Exclamation of surprise or dismay, possibly from *spasimo (di) Dio*.
[22] Old Tuscan form of the past part., sync. of *trovato*.
[23] 'Nincompoops', conceited and hollow-minded person, dim. of *forame*, little hole.
[24] Metathesis of *vagheggiare*, to court.
[25] Euph. alteration of *diavolo*.
[26] Become aware, old Tuscan comp. of *dare*.
[27] Euph. for *in fe' di Dio*.
[28] 'Go to the beggars', get lost.
[29] To reprimand, to make sb. face the music, zetacized comp. of the notes *sol* and *fa*.
[30] 'More confounded than the church music of the Armenians', as in the Armenian songs of the former Church of San Basilio in Florence.
[31] 'Offensive jest', possibly from *bisca*, gambling hall.
[32] 'To tread with caution', lit. to put on shoes of lead.
[33] As in: curiosity killed the cat.
[34] Who spoils the pleasure of others.
[35] 'While I dissemble like the cat of Masino', idiom.
[36] Somebody who plays ignorant, see *Introduction*, n. 220.
[37] 'I am sharp-sighted', discerning.
[38] I have seen the world, lit. 'I have pissed in more than one snow.'
[39] To school.
[40] Tongue, lit. a strip of leather.
[41] 'Chittering gossips', see *cicala* above, n. 13.
[42] 'Muckraker', lit. oven sweep.

I — *Equivoco sopra il sonetto con la coda*

Questi sonetti, o Tina, ch'i' ho composto,
me gl'ha dettati una Musa buffona,
cantando d'improviso alla carlona[1]
sul suono, spinto dal calor del mosto.

E s'io fo[2] mal, facc'egli: i' son disposto
così di metter la poesia in canzona;
or tu guarda a colui che te gli dona,
non al presente ch'è di poco costo.

Sol per tuo amor gl'ho fatti, e scritti in fretta,
non perché il mondo me ne doni loda,
ch'i' non curo l'allor su la berretta.

Quest'altra volta, perché più tu goda,
dacché se' larga di natura, aspetta
da me tutti i sonetti con la coda.

[1] Folksily, with ref. to the old times of *Re Carlone*, Charlemagne.
[2] Tuscan form for *faccio*; cf. above, *Nencio alla Tina*, n. 12.

II — *Sopra l'alzar lo stile*

Tina, i' so legger bene e rilevato
la storia di Liombruno[1] e Josaffatte,[2]
sebben, per esser nato in queste fratte,[3]
sotto il maestro mai non sono stato.

E il Sere del Dificio[4] m'ha giurato,
quand'egli ha visto le poesie ch'i' ho fatte,
ch'elle son belle, e i piedi in terra batte,
e vuol ch'i' mi sia a Pisa[5] addottorato.

Io canto quand'i' son ben ben satollo
sul chitarrin, con boce[6] sì sottile
ch'io ne disgrado insin maestro Apollo.

Vieni un poco da me Tina gentile,
ché s'egli avvien che tu mi segga in collo,
mi sentirai ben tosto[7] alzar lo stile.

---

[1] Eponymous character of an anon. fourteenth-century *cantare*.
[2] Jewish king; it was believed that the Last Judgement would happen in the Valley of Josaphat.
[3] In the thicket, in dire straits.
[4] Judge of the criminal court, apheresis of *edificio*.
[5] In the burlesque vocabulary 'Pisa' stands for the female sexual organ, perhaps with ref. to its Etruscan meaning of 'morass'; cf. below, Sonnet XLI.
[6] Old Tuscan form for *voce*.
[7] Promptly, literary Gallicism, but vernacular adj. means hard.

III — *Sopra il brodo di castrato*[1]

Queste disgrazie non si danno a patti,[2]
Tina, tu hai la febbre e la trascuri,
né par che della vita tu ti curi,
come il morir sia baia:[3] oh, siam noi matti?

Non bisogna indugiar, quand'un dà i tratti,[4]
a medicarsi, acciò che il mal non duri;
tu non mangi e non bei,[5] né t'assicuri
sopra i medicamenti ch'i' t'ho fatti.

I' ho cotto una lacchetta[6] di castrato
e fatto una pappina acconcia in modo
che il pizzicor ti metterà al palato.

Ma che tu ingozzi il mannerin[7] non lodo:
basta, se hai stomacuzzo raffreddato,
che tu lo poppi, e poi ti bea il brodo.

[1] Wether.
[2] 'Do not grant terms to sickness', the consequences of these ailments cannot be foreseen.
[3] Joke, bagatelle, aph. of *abbaiare*.
[4] Convulsions, spasms.
[5] Tuscan sync. form of *bevi*, with loss of intervocalic 'v' as in the Eng. word 'beer'.
[6] Leg fillet, dim. of *lacca*, from Lat. *lacertus*.
[7] Morsel of wether meat, from Lat. *mannarium*.

IV — *Sopra il mal del granchio*[1]

O Tina, i' sento dalla gente dire
che il mal del granchio spesso ti dà noia,
e che allor par che tu tiri le cuoia,
raggrinzi tutta, e mostri di basire.[2]

Non 'gna[3] farsene beffe, egl'è un martìre[4]
che a risico si va ch'un se ne muoia:
i' ho un medicamento ch'é una gioia,
e presto senza duol ti vo guarire.

Quest'è un anel dov'è della gran bestia
un pezzo d'ugna, e possoti bel bello
con esso liberar d'ogni molestia.

Porgimi il dito, Tina, eccolo, vello:
se vuoi che il granchio parta, con modestia
lascia ch'io te lo metta nell'anello.

---

[1] Cramps, pop. alteration of *crampo*, here with ref. to the saying *cavare un granchio dalla buca*.
[2] Faint, Tuscan word.
[3] Dialectal aph. of *bisogna*.
[4] Suffering.

V — *Sopra l'arista[1] e la salsiccia*

Stasera, o Tina, ch'egli è carnesciale[2]
e che a pusigno[3] invitansi i parenti,
tu che macini bene a due palmenti,[4]
se vien da me non se' per istar male.

I' ho messo con del pepe e con del sale,
con uve passe ed altri condimenti,
una vivanda da allegarti i denti
a fuoco or in un pentol badiale.[5]

Quest'è una fetta d'arista amorosa
ed un po' di salsiccia col finocchio,[6]
che non sentisti mai la miglior cosa.

E perché tu non m'abbi a far malocchio
e gridar che la carne sia tigliosa,[7]
l'arista torrò io, tu torrai 'l rocchio.[8]

---

[1] Pork loin.
[2] Tuscan form for *carnevale*, from *carne lasciare*.
[3] Late light meal, lit. after dinner, from Vulg. Lat. *postcenium*.
[4] Eat avidly, lit. grind on both sides.
[5] 'In a kettle as big as a convent's'.
[6] Florentine derog. term used as a syn. for sodomite, with possible ref. to the phrase *mettere il finocchio fra le mele*, lit. to serve fennel with apples after a meal.
[7] Gristly, lit. fibrous like a lime tree.
[8] The roll, i.e. the sausage, from Lat. *rotulus*.

VI — *Sopra la beccheria*

Tina, ogni volta che tu va' al macello
per qualche lonza,[1] questo tuo beccaio,[2]
ch'è un tentennone,[3] rubati il danaio
e un gran pezzo ti dà di tarantello.[4]

So che non tocca a me la cosa, e paio
prosontuoso, ma per ben favello:
vuo' tu esser di costui dunque il zimbello,[5]
come gl'uccei presicci al paretaio?[6]

Tina, va' a casa, e di' a tua ma'[7] in un tratto:
puttanaccia di me, se mi mandate
più per la carne i' la vo dare al gatto;

poi di' forte a tuo pa': non vi crediate
ch'io vi voglia più andare a nessun patto,
se sopra voi la beccheria non fate.

---

[1] Loin cuts, but esp. in Tuscany the oxtail.
[2] The butcher's, but with ref. to *becco*, derog. for cuckold.
[3] 'Fumbler', deverbal from *tentennare*.
[4] Lower-quality cut of meat added as an extra, lit. tuna sausage typical of the city of Taranto.
[5] See *Introduction*, beginning of section 4.
[6] Fowling net.
[7] Apocope of *madre*, like *pa'* for *padre*.

VII — *Sopra il montar sul fico*

Tina, questo tuo fico castagnuolo[1]
è così liscio, e i rami ha così alti,
che l'adoprar le mani e i piè non valti
per andar com'uccello in vetta a volo.

Tu se' per starci tutto il dì a piuolo,[2]
or con lacci provandoti or con salti,
e non far altro al fin di tanti assalti
che sudar senz'alzarsi un piè dal suolo.

Ma sta', che farti un tal servizio i' posso:
so ben il modo com'e' vi si sale;
sta' allegra, Tina, or or te lo do scosso.

Abbassa il capo e appoggialo al pedale,[3]
ché se fai ponte, e ch'io ti salga addosso,
vi monterò ben su senz'altre scale.

[1] Variety of fig tree with small chestnut-like fruits.
[2] 'As if pegged.'
[3] Lower part of the trunk.

VIII — *Sopra il tessere*

Tina, quel panno che tu m'hai tessuto
è floscio, sì che al tasto ei non si sente,
cresposo e rado come un filondente[1]
mal ordito, mal fatto, e mal tenuto.

Tirar le casse[2] a te non hai saputo
in quel che il cannellin[3] sfilar si sente,
o il male dal tener la tela lente,
o dal tirar le calcole[4] è venuto;

o dal pettin, che or non è più stretto
com'era già quand'un po' po' bagnato
tutto l'ordito entrava e usciva netto.

Ora il tempo te l'ha tanto allargato
che a far che il fil riempia il canaletto
vuol esser con la crusca imbozzimato.[5]

---

[1] Open-weave cotton fabric used for embroidery, from *filo in dente*, lit. woven with one yarn for each tooth of the comb that spaces the warp, syn. of *canovaccio*.
[2] Loom.
[3] 'Little bobbin', dim. of *canna*, little cylinder for the filling yarn.
[4] The treadles of the loom.
[5] To apply a viscous solution of boiled bran to make a yarn thicker and smoother, from late Lat. *apozema*, decoction.

IX — *Sopra il rizzarsi*

Tina mia bella, quando tu lagori
nel campo e che il padron ti viene intorno,
ti rizzi[1] a un tratto e poi gli dai 'l buongiorno,
e ti fai 'n viso di mille colori.

Ma non si fan già a me questi favori,
e pur sei volte il dì parto e ritorno:
'gna ch'i' sia proprio qualche perdigiorno,
dacché tu non ti rizzi e non m'onori.

Chi è ben creata,[2] come si conviene,
rizzasi a tutti; a me il can mi s'aizza
per più dispetto, e voltansi le rene.

Può far il cielo![3] I' ho pur la grande stizza:
che differenza c'è tra lui e mene,[4]
che al padron sempre e a me mai non si rizza?

[1] Rise, denom. from Lat. *rectus*, erect.
[2] 'Well-mannered', cognate of *creanza*, from old Sp. *criar*, to raise.
[3] 'By heav'n!'
[4] Old Tuscan form of the acc. pers. pron. *me* with unstressed clitic *-ne*, possibly interrogative in origin.

X — *Sopra la gammurra*[1]

Le donne la gammurra oggi si fanno,
recipiente agl'anni ed allo stato:
chi di rovescio e chi d'accordellato,[2]
Tina mia bella, e chi d'un altro panno.

Molte col pelo e molte senza l'hanno,
di perpignano[3] s'usano un buondato;[4]
ma quelle di rovescio accotonato,
più bel veder ma minor util danno.

A me mi par che sia degna di loda,
e più da quei ch'hanno la man callosa,
quella ch'è liscia e di pannina soda,

che para l'acqua, e quand'ella è fangosa
si netta. Ond'io gridar vo'[5] ch'ognun m'oda:
la tua mi piace, ché non è pelosa!

---

[1] Women's open-fronted overgarment, often without sleeves but lined with fur, possibly cognate of *zimarra*, a garment lined with sable fur.
[2] Rep, denom. from *corda*.
[3] Low-quality wool fabric originally from Perpignan.
[4] In abundance.
[5] Apoc. of *voglio*.

XI — *Sopra il ber l'uova*

Tina, ho veduto che quando tu hai male
cuocer ti fa tua ma' sotto la brace
un uovo fresco, e non si può dar pace
se non l'ingoi bazzotto[1] e senza sale.

E tu fai da svogliata e l'hai per male,
ma all'appipito[2] poi non ti dispiace,
sì che a un tratto risani, e più vivace
mostri quella tua faccia imperiale.

Tua ma' è avara, ché s'i' fussi lei,
quando la febbre ti manuca e stroppia,[3]
più presto e meglio assai ti guarirei.

Perché non far la medicina doppia?
Deh,[4] vien da me quando malata sei,
ché, se vorrai, te no darò una coppia.

[1] Soft-boiled.
[2] Tuscan pop. form for *appetito*.
[3] Cripples, metathesis of *storpiare*.
[4] Resigned exclamation introducing a plea or a wish, from Lat. *deus*.

XII — *Sopra l'infornar il pane*

Ieri il pan che al padron, Tina, infornasti,
perch'era tondo e di gran bianco tutto
venne dentro, e di fuor cotto e rasciutto,
e in somma tal che tu lo contentasti.

Ma il mio, perch'era a picce,[1] lo lasciasti
ardere in mo'[2] ch'io non ne cavo frutto.
Forse è sì male stagionato e brutto,
perché alla peggio il forno tuo spazzasti.

Tu mi risponderai che questo avviene
perché il suo me'[3] s'inforna; e i' ti rispondo
che i buon bocconi piaccion anche a mene.

E da qua innanzi anch'io (poter del mondo!),[4]
perché tu me l'inforni e cuoca bene
voglio ancor io, come il padron, il tondo.

---

[1] Pair of breads joint on one side, deverb. from *appicciare*, to put together.
[2] Apoc. of *modo*.
[3] Apoc. of *meglio*.
[4] 'By all that's holy!'

XIII — *Sopra il sonar lo zufolo*

Tina, più volte m'hai detto e ridetto,
quando nel bosco i' sto guardando i buoi,
che maggior gusto al mondo aver non puoi
che sentirmi sonar quel zufoletto.

Se da me vieni un giorno, i' ti prometto
più sonate insegnarti che non vuoi;
prima sonerò io ben bene, e poi
ti porrò in mano un zufolo perfetto.

Il suono è bello, ma non creder mica[1]
che quella boce,[2] che sì ben rintocca,
s'impari mai senza durar fatica.

Sempre nel buco col dito si tocca,
ma il tutto sta, se vuoi ch'io te lo dica,
nel saper tener ben la lingua in bocca.

---

[1] At all, neg. intensifier, lit. breadcrumb.
[2] Dialectal alteration of *voce*.

XIV — *Sopra il pescar i granchi*

T'ho preso questa zucca[1] e questa zappa[2]
per cercarti due granchi tenerelli,
Tina, quaggiù per questi borratelli[3]
dove chi sa pescar molti n'acchiappa.

A me di rado e pochi me ne scappa,
ché sprezzo i morsi e piglio i brutti e i belli;
e s'egl'è vero, senza io ne favelli,
il padron lo può dir che se li pappa.

Ma se la luna è scema[4] (oh, caso strano!)
dentro son vuoti, e il guscio solamente,
quand'un ne pigli, ti rimane in mano.

Tina, tu che se' astrologa eccellente,
fammi veder, perch'i' non peschi invano,
se la luna ora è scema o se è crescente.

[1] Gourd used as a float.
[2] Type of fishing net, mainly used for fishing lampreys.
[3] Ditches, dim. of *borro*.
[4] Waning.

XV — *Sopra il rassettar serrami*[1]

Il tuo macinatoio ha ogni serrame
per la vecchiaia rugginoso e guasto,
e se la prova vuoi veder, va' al tasto;
e s'io dico bugie, dimmi poi infame.

Se rassettar lo vuoi senza che chiame
i magnan,[2] che son asin senza basto,[3]
vien per me, che sì ben l'acconcio e impasto
che tutti i ladri si morrian di fame.

Queste man per tanaglia e per martello
mi servon tanto ben, che senza troppa
fatica appicco e spicco il bolcinello.[4]

Tu dirai poi ch'i' sia d'oro una coppa,
s'io ti metto di dietro il chiavistello
e t'ungo la stanghetta della toppa.[5]

[1] On fixing locks.
[2] Locksmiths, from Vulg. Lat. *maninus*, handyman.
[3] 'Jackass without a bit', lit. without a saddle.
[4] 'Pick the staple and pin', Sienese alteration of *boncinello*.
[5] Keyhole, possibly from *toppo*, stump.

XVI — *Sopra il dormire scoperta*

Tina, tu dormi sola in sul saccone,[1]
senza di questa brezza aver paura;
e perché t'hai cattiva diacitura,[2]
butti in terra il lenzuol spesso e il coltrone.[3]

Io veramente n'ho compassione,
che, mentre sta scoperta una creatura,
può beccarsi su ben qualche freddura
e in quattro giorni andarsene al cassone.[4]

Se tu vieni a diacer nel mio stramaccio,[5]
ancor che caschi un panno ch'io v'ho grosso,
non avrai di ricoprirti impaccio,

ch'io ti ricoprirone il me' ch'io posso;
e se non val la coltrice e il piumaccio,[6]
mi ti porrò sin con la vita addosso.

---

[1] Straw mattress.
[2] Tuscan alteration of *giacitura*, lying position.
[3] Soft padded blanket, aug. of *coltre*.
[4] Coffin.
[5] 'Bed of down', from *strame*, bedding straw.
[6] Feather pillow.

XVII — *Sopra il menare*[1] *il bue*

Vien'oltre, o Tina, e' m'è scappato il bue
e a rompicollo va per quella stoppia:
ohchoi![2] vedi s'e' corre? Egli si stroppia
se da que' greppi[3] tombola all'ingiue.[4]

Almen questo ch'ho in man mena un po' tue,
tanto che con quell'altro il[5] giunga in coppia.
Venga l'assillo[6] insin ch'ei non iscoppia!
Diluviate disgrazie, eccene piue?

Io non mi curo ch'e' mi sia menato
quand'i' ho tempo e posso far di meno,
ché veramente mi par un peccato.

Ma or, tanto che gl'esca quel veleno,
se menar non lo vuoi, tienlo legato,
perché a casa da me poi me lo meno.

---

[1] To lead by hand, from late Lat. *minare*, to prod cattle; cf. below, Sonnet XXI. 1, in the sense of stirring a dish.
[2] Interjection expressing commotion and concern.
[3] Slippery slopes.
[4] Rhyming alteration of *all'ingiù*; same alterations below for *tue* (*tu*) and *piue* (*più*).
[5] Old alternate form of m. obj. pron. *lo*, apoc. of Lat. *ille*.
[6] Horsefly, hence torment.

XVIII — *Sopra lo scodar le galline*

Tu hai scodate tutte le galline,
Tina, perché le facciano più uova,
ma tu te n'avvedrai presto alla prova
che in zeri torneranti le decine.[1]

Tu l'hai malconce sì le poverine,
ch'erbe ch'elle si becchin lor non giova;
questa ricetta scritta i' non l'ho trova,
e ho letto un libro dal principio al fine.

Oh, ora sì che sterili saranno!
Va', di' che pur un tuorlo tu ne goda,
e se tu hai fatto il mal sarà tuo danno.

In cambio d'acquistarti utile e loda,
tu ne sei per star mal tutto questo anno,
perché l'uova non ha chi non ha coda.

---

[1] 'For zero returns will prove slim pickin's', lit. your tens will turn up in zeros.

XIX — *Sopra l'imbottare*

I' arei[1] bisogno, Tina, or ch'e' s'imbotta
questo poco di vin che s'è raccolto,
perché il mio peverin[2] m'è stato tolto,
oggi della tua pevera a buon'otta.[3]

Ma i' sento dir ch'ella è si mal condotta,
ch'ella non ne ritien poco né molto;
i' vorrei ben saper chi è quello stolto
che con sì poca grazia te l'ha rotta.

Tu sai che prima, quando la[4] teneva,
la ti sarà prestandola scommessa,
meco[5] tutta la gente ti diceva.

Or che farai, ch'ella non par più dessa?[6]
Pazza che se', bastar pur ti doveva
salvarla allor che tu l'avevi fessa.

---

[1] Sync. of *avrei*; on the loss of intervocalic 'v' cf. above, Sonnet III, n. 5.
[2] Wooden funnel, dim. of *pevera*.
[3] Old literary form of *ora*, perhaps from Lat. *quota (hora est?)*, by aph. and consonant doubling.
[4] Aph. of third pers. f. pron. *ella*.
[5] With me, from Lat. *mecum*; cf. *teco* below, Sonnet XX. 9.
[6] The same, literary form of third pers. demonstr. pron. *essa (stessa)*, from Lat. *id ipsum*.

XX — *Sopra il cavar il grillo*

Tutta la gente va a Monte Morello,[1]
Tina, doman che vi si fa la festa
de' grilli,[2] e a casa pur un sol non resta
o di Campi, o di Sesto, o di Castello.[3]

Anch'io vo' andar, se però il tempo è bello,
che non c'è fiera più nobil di questa;
se ancor tu vieni, andrem qua per la pesta,[4]
tu sulla ciuca,[5] ed io sull'asinello.

Ma to'[6] una gabbia teco, e i' con lo spillo,
o con un fuscel lungo in man ch'i' abbia,
del buco fuor farò scappare il grillo.

Tiri pur calci e sputi per la rabbia,
perch'ei t'insegni a mezza notte il trillo,
vivo lo caccerò nella tua gabbia.

---

[1] Mountain northwest of Florence.
[2] 'Festival of Crickets', traditionally celebrated on Ascension Day.
[3] Villages around Florence.
[4] Well-trodden way, deverb. from *pestare*.
[5] 'She-ass.'
[6] Apoc. of imperative form *togli*, take.

XXI — *Sopra la faverella*[1]

S'io ti veggo menar la faverella,
Tina, anch'io tutto quanto mi dimeno,[2]
e per dolcezza quasi vengo meno,
sentendo il cuor che dentro mi saltella.

Ne ingoierei da me una metadella,[3]
e vorrei sempre averne il corpo pieno;
l'altre civaie,[4] ancor che buone sieno,
mi van tra la camicia e la gonnella.[5]

Par ch'i' esca della Torre della Fame,[6]
in modo l'appipito mi si drizza
quando scoperto mostrimi il tegame.

Ma tu mi fai venir la grande stizza,[7]
in quel punto (se avvien che alcun ti chiame)
che fai per fretta che fuor l'olio schizza.

[1] Porridge of boiled fava beans.
[2] I flounce about; cf. below, Sonnet XXXVI. 14, in the sense of wagging the tail.
[3] Old unit of measure for liquids corresponding to half a flask, from *metà*.
[4] Foods, from Lat. *cibaria*.
[5] Without appetite, lit. between the shirt and the smock.
[6] Famous tower in Pisa where, in 1289, Count Ugolino was imprisoned with two of his sons and two grandsons, and starved to death, as told by Dante in *Inf.* XXXIII.
[7] Anger, from Lat. *titio*, firebrand.

XXII — *Sopra il ripescar la secchia*

Io ti sentii gridar ier con la vecchia
mentr'ero al campo a seminar le vecce,[1]
e quasi v'acciuffaste per le trecce,
perché nel pozzo ti cascò la secchia.

Scusala, ell'è caparbia perché invecchia
e aspetta dalla morte aver le frecce;
e tu, ch'ha' da competer le cortecce,
alle sue grida non prestare orecchia.

Or, se la secchia t'è cascata in fondo
senza manico avere e senza nocchio,[2]
non è per questo rovinato il mondo:

io ch'ho gl'oncin, senza tenerti a crocchio,[3]
tanto frugando andrò giù nel profondo
che te l'infilerò giusto nell'occhio.

[1] Vetch.
[2] Knob, possibly from Lat. *nux*, nut.
[3] In idle conversation.

XXIII — *Sopra le pesche*

Tina, ier l'altro nel mio castagneto
battei dai ricci non so che marroni,
e me n'empiei le tasche de' calzoni
per farti quattro succiole[1] in segreto.

Ma Ciapin tuo fratel, ch'è un indiscreto,
vedendomi lontano andare aioni,[2]
pigliando il tempo (oh ve',[3] che discrezioni!)
mi scosse il pesco ch'i' ho dall'uscio dreto.[4]

Ma se non era per tuo amore, il ghiotto
me le posava quivi fresche fresche,
e guai a lui s'io mel cacciavo sotto.

Tu sai ch'io non comporto simil tresche,
e ch'io son uomo scorrubbiato e rotto,[5]
e ch'io vo' torre e non vo' dar le pesche.

---

[1] 'Chestnut suckers', chestnuts boiled with the skin on.
[2] Tuscan idiom for wandering around.
[3] Excl. apoc. of *vedi*.
[4] Old alternate form of *dietro*, from Lat. *de retro*.
[5] Short-tempered and seasoned.

XXVI — *Sopra il far la gramigna*[1]

O Tina, se no' andiam sotto la vigna
da quel divelto di viti d'Albano,[2]
porta la cesta ed una marra[3] in mano,
ch'i' vo' che noi facciam della gramigna.

Non vo' ch'abbia a gridar la tua matrigna
che la giornata tu consumi in vano:
con essa piena tornerai pian piano,
ond'ella non farà la cera arcigna.[4]

Tu zappandola ben la netterai
della terra, e po'[5] a me, che nella gora[6]
te la lavi ben ben, la porgerai.

E tratta poi ben risciacquata fuora,
al mulo del padron dar la potrai,
che più manuca assai che non lagora.

---

[1] Dog's-tooth or couch-grass, from Lat. *gramen*, grass.
[2] Mountain south-west of Florence.
[3] Pull hoe or pick.
[4] 'Sour and cold countenance', from Fr. *rechigner*, to show the teeth.
[5] Apoc. of *poi*.
[6] Irrigation canal.

XXVII — *Sopra il seccar la peschiera*

Tina mia cara, oggi il padron m'ha detto
che in tutti e' modi vuol che questa sera
si voti[1] affatto e secchi la peschiera,
per far dei pesci non so che banchetto.

Io, che non posso metterl'ad effetto
s'un non m'aiuta o mostra la maniera,
perché so quanto in questo tu se' fiera,
stasera meco in compagnia t'aspetto.

Scalzo e sbracciato quivi i' mi riduco,
e come l'acqua sarà un po' calata
farò vederti se quei pesci i' sbuco.

Tu starai con la rete spalancata
a me dinanzi, mentre i' sturo il buco,
a ricever i pesci alla cascata.

---

[1] Drain, denom. from *vuoto* with Tuscan generalized monophthong.

XXVIII — *Sopra il dar bere ai castroni*[1]

I' veggo, o Tina, il tuo castron brinato[2]
sempre dal branco andarsene lontano;
tu dovresti, s'egli cieco è nato,
quando e' bisogna pur menarlo a mano.

Né ti dovrebbe già parere strano
far quest'ufficio, essendo egli malato:
sai che l'ingratitudine è un peccato
che il prete vuol che noi 'l tenghiam lontano.

Sarebbe d'una donna atto gentile
menarlo al fonte, prima che a diacere
con l'altre bestie andasse nell'ovile;

e se non ti scostassi dal dovere
vedresti, ancor che un animal sia vile,
ch'è carità menar un cieco a bere.

[1] Aug. of *castrato*, see above Sonnet III.
[2] Brindled.

XXIX — *Sopra il mangiar l'agnello*

Ogn'or che con le pecore in pastura
quinentro vo ne' sodi[1] del Vivuola,[2]
sempre qualcuna il lupo me n'imbola[3]
e se la porta via senza paura.

Ma ieri l'acchiappai, per mia ventura,
che appunto avea un agnel quasi che in gola,
e fattogli col cane una gran fola,[4]
glielo feci posar sulla verdura.

Eccolo, o Tina, scorticato e netto:
portalo a casa e cuocinelo tosto,
ch'una cena farem com'un banchetto.

Dar le parti dinanzi a te ho proposto,
le rigaglie[5] a comun sieno e il guazzetto,
e per me tor quelle di dietro arrosto.

[1] Untilled fields, from Lat. *solidus.*
[2] Family name; see below, Sonnet XXXIX. 4.
[3] Tuscan alteration of *involare*, to snatch away like birds of prey, from *volare* with illative prefix.
[4] Throng, cognate of *folla.*
[5] Giblets, probably from Lat. *regalia*, (morsels) fit for a king.

XXX — *Sopra il versar della botte*

Tina mia bella, i' so che la tua botte,
dov'unguanno[1] imbottato hai l'acquerello,[2]
(canchigna!)[3] tutto il ber manda in bordello,[4]
perché gocciola forte e giorno e notte.

Chiamami, perch'io vengo a tutte l'otte
a ristuccarla senz'oprar coltello;
purché non sia squarciato lo sportello,
muffato il fondo, e sien le doghe rotte.

Ti turerò ogni buco ed ogni fesso,
o Tina, in carità, perch'io non faccio
questi servizi mai per interesse.

E mentre stoppa[5] per di dietro caccio,
dinanzi metterò in un tempo istesso
una cannella ch'è com'il mio braccio.

---

[1] This year, from Lat. *hocque anno.*
[2] Watery wine obtained from the leftover grape pressings, dim. of *acqua.*
[3] Interj. expressing grief and aggravation, possibly sync. of *cancherigna*, from *canchero.*
[4] 'All the drink goes off to ruin.'
[5] Oakum.

XXXI — *Sopra il susin torto*

Tina, quel mio susin che nel divelto[1]
unguanno fu da me sotterra fitto,
e ch'i' avea pel più bello e il più diritto
tra cento e più rimessiticci[2] scelto,

dove prima venìa disteso e svelto[3]
col capo all'erta,[4] ora si piega afflitto,
in modo tal ch'i', dal dolor trafitto,
poco men che da terra or non l'ho svelto.

Né trovo modo o via ch'egli si arrenda,
ché s'io lo lego al pal con le ritorte[5]
mi par sempre veder ch'e' si scoscenda.[6]

Tu sola il puoi risuscitar da morte,
ch'hai nelle mani una virtù stupenda
che fa drizzar tutte le cose torte.

---

[1] 'New-dug plot.'
[2] Shoots, from past part. *rimesso*, regenerated (after pruning).
[3] Equivocal rhyme: limber, but below (l. 8) it means uprooted.
[4] 'With head held high', from Lat. *erigere*.
[5] Withies.
[6] As if it snaps, from Lat. *conscindere*, to break off, with augm. prefix *s-*.

XXXII — *Sopra il lavorar l'orto*

Tina, tu vieni a lavorarmi l'orto
con la tua marra, e zappi sì di rado
ch'io te ne so, per dirtela, il mal grado,
e quasi a male stento lo comporto.[1]

E se non fussi che rispetto i' porto
(perdinci!)[2] a tutto quanto il parentado,
te la torre' di man quand'io ci bado,
perch'i' conosco che tu mi fai torto.

Non vedi che profitto alcun non fai
e butti il seme via col lavorio,
sebben ti fai tener donna d'assai?[3]

Deh, lascia star che molto me' poss'io
lagorar con la zappa che, vedrai,
il tuo giardino a te, che tu a me il mio.

---

[1] Literary syn. of *sopporto*.
[2] Euph. alteration of *per Dio*.
[3] Of many qualities, competent and confident.

XXXIII — *Sopra la golpe*[1]

Ieri nel mio pollaio entrò la golpe,
allargando l'imposta alla finestra
fatta di pruno, vetrice e ginestra,
e d'un cappon mangiò l'ossa e le polpe.

Ma voglio che il padron me solo incolpe
s'un dì non gli fo recer[2] la minestra;
l'acchiapperò ben io, sia furba e destra,
e questa sconterà con l'altre colpe.

Presa ch'io l'averò farem cavelle,[3]
o Tina, andando per la vicinanza
l'uova accattare, e mostrerem la pelle;

e la sera, tornati alla mia stanza,
la metà n'averai delle più belle,
sebben d'un paio io so che te n'avanza.

---

[1] Tuscan alteration of *volpe*; cf. above, *Nencio alla Tina*, n. 9.
[2] Regurgitate, from Lat. *reicere*.
[3] A little something, from Lat. *quam velles*, what you want.

XXXIV — *Sopra il mangiar le fave*

I' t'ho veduto manicare[1] in fretta
fave marzuole, e tanto aprir la bocca
che, ben ch'una per volta ve ne metta,
ella va in corpo e nessun lato tocca.

Gl'è una vergogna ed è una cosa sciocca
che non sta bene ad una giovinetta,
che, se non è la mamma che t'imbocca,
tu non la sai accomodare stretta.

Già che la gente non era sì astuta,
in queste cose la non si guardava;
ma oggidì pare ch'ogni cosa puta.[2]

Imperò, Tina mia, se non ti grava,
quando tu ti satolli e se' veduta,
aprila tanto che v'entri una fava.

---

[1] Same as *manucare*, see *Nencio alla Tina*, n. 7.
[2] Everything seems distasteful, from Lat. *putere*, to stink.

XXXV — *Sopra il nibbio*

Tina, ve' il nibbio che si cala, olà![1]
Senti la chioccia che grida clo-clo,
perché i pulcini ricoprir non può
con l'alie or ch'ei sen vanno e qui e qua.

Va' là gridando: sciocà, sciocà,[2] va'!
Tu non ti muovi, tu non gridi, ohibò![3]
Ecco, già n'ha preso uno, un altro, ohchò![4]
Il branco questa volta scemerà.

Di' un po': quest'anno come darai tu
i capponi al padron, Tina, e da che
trarrai dodici serque[5] d'uova e più?

Io non ci vo' pensare; in quanto a me,
ti dico sol che, s'egli vien quassù,
tutto il peso sarà sopra di te.

---

[1] Excl. to draw attention, comp. of *oh* and *là*.
[2] Expressive interjection to chase away chickens, nowadays in the short form *sciò*.
[3] Excl. of disapproval and dismay, comp. of *ohi* and the sound symbol *bò*, expressing disbelief.
[4] See above, Sonnet XVII, n. 2.
[5] Dozens.

XXXVI — *Sopra il cane*

Talvolta i' sto a veder, Tina mia bella,
quando a ruzzar[1] tu te ne stai col cane,
e che gli metti in bocca il cacio o il pane
e ti lasci leccar sin la scodella,

che il zotico[2] sta mogio e non saltella,
né ti fa festa con maniere umane;
anzi, abbaiando con boccacce strane,
or ti morde la scarpa or la gonnella.

Deh, se in quel cane io fussi trasformato,
verrei ben tosto a succiar su la broda,
quando con quel te' te'[3] fussi chiamato;

lascerei gl'ossi e ogn'altra cosa soda,
e quando io fussi poi ben satollato,
ti stare' innanzi a dimenar la coda.

---

[1] To play with animals, chasing and tumbling about, also in the obscene sense as in the name Ruzzante.
[2] Rude and oafish, perhaps by apheresis from late Lat. *idioticus*.
[3] Interj. used to call an animal to eat its food, apoc. of Lat. *tene*, take.

XXXVII — *Sopra il dar le noci*

Tutto il popolo grida a viva boce
ch'io sono un ingrataccio e un ignorante,
perché quel giorno ch'io battei le noce
non te le messi innanzi tutte quante.

Tu sai ch'io dissi: pigliatene tante,
che tu non m'abbia a metter poi più in croce;
ma s'io non sono ad empierti bastante
la sporta, il male a me molto più cuoce.

Tina, tu l'hai, per dirtela, sì grande
ch'un come me mendico si sconforta
a poter l'empier da tutte le bande.[1]

Però con pazienza tel comporta,
se tu non vuoi riempierla di ghiande,
chè per me troppo larga è la tua sporta.

---

[1] To fill it up, lit. from all sides.

XXXVIII — *Sopra il popone*[1]

I' vo a Firenze, o Tina, dal padrone
per veder se del gran[2] mi vuol prestare,
e perch'io non ho altro da portare
va' un po' nel campo e recami un popone.

Ma lo vorrei di tutta perfezione,
grosso, di peso e con le fette rare,
ch'è diffıcil poterlo contentare,
essendo ch'egli è un uom senza ragione.

E' non è avvezzo a far troppe parole:
se non lo trova di tutto sapore,
sempre nel capo batter me lo suole.

Guarda dunque ch'ei sia di buon odore,
nato e cresciuto a dove batte il sole,
e abbia grosso picciuolo e largo fiore.

[1] Melon, from Lat. *pepo*.
[2] Money, lit. grain.

XXXIX — *Sopra l'annaffiar l'orto*

Tina, con quella gralzia[1] che tu suoli,
ieri, nell'annaffiarmi l'orto, a caso
con un urto rompestimi quel vaso
dov'era il re di tutti i miei vivuoli.[2]

Ma apponla a me,[3] se un dì non te duoli
e non arricci per la stizza il naso,
ch'io ti vo romper quel che ti è rimaso
intero e saldo a dov'il ranno[4] coli.

Ovver la vília[5] di Pasqua di Ceppo,[6]
quando tu vieni a chiedermi il danaio,[7]
dirò di no, bench'io ne fussi zeppo;

e con bel modo, per colmar lo staio,[8]
mentre chiedi la mancia a piè del greppo,[9]
io spaccherotti il tuo salvadanaio.

---

[1] Literary alteration of *grazia*.
[2] Violet plants, from an old form of *viola*.
[3] 'Charge me', lit. put it (i.e. the blame) on me.
[4] Lye.
[5] Sync. form of *vigilia*.
[6] Christmas, also called *Pasqua della Natività*; the *ceppo* was a hollow log (cf. Fr. *tronc*) used as an alms box, whose pieces were distributed after the collection to be burned at home on Christmas Eve.
[7] Old alternate form of *denaro*, as below in *salvadanaio* (l. 14).
[8] For good measure; old dry measure, esp. for grains, from Lat. *sextarius*.
[9] Alteration of *greppia*, manger; cf. above, Sonnet XVII. 4.

XL — *Sopra il sonar il cembalo*

Tina, tu mi fai rider quando vai
cantando il maggio[1] a questi contadini
e suoni un cembal senza dinderlini,[2]
cosa in contado non usata mai.

Tu vedi ben che sì poc'uova fai
che non darian le spese a due mucini;
anzi, ridon di te tutti i vicini,
ché di saper suonar credi e non sai.

Tale stormento a te non si conviene,
e poco giova quel tuo dagli-dagli[3]
se quei cosi vi mancan che fan bene.

Invan, Tina, t'affanni e ti travagli:
non è tua colpa, il mancamento viene
sol perché come me non hai i sonagli.

[1] Spring songs traditionally sung on the first Sunday of May, also called *maggiolata*.
[2] 'Tambourine without jingles', onomatopoeic, but *dindi* is a childish word for money.
[3] 'Thump-thumps.'

XLI — *Sopra il pescar pei pantani*

Tina, colà nella mollaia[1] vota
mess'ho la man sotto una pietra fessa,
e morso stato son da una granchiessa
ch'ha figliato testé tra quella mota.

Che i granchi abbian due bocche[2] è cosa nota,
ed io balordo pur la man v'ho messa,
e il sangue (ohimè!) di gocciolar non cessa,
né giova ch'io la succi o ch'io la scuota.

Or mi sovviene (e ci fu Meo di Cecco)[3]
quanto mi disse al Tetto dei pisani[4]
un ch'aveva un barbon come il mio becco:

veggo a un segno, diss'ei, ch'hai nelle mani,
che tu se' per pigliar dei granchi a secco,
però non pescar troppo pei pantani.

[1] Same as *pantano*, morass, from *molle*.
[2] Claws.
[3] Fam. dim. of Bartolomeo and Francesco.
[4] Building erected by Pisan prisoners after 1364 in Piazza della Signoria, where there were the post-office, market stalls, and the earliest gatherings of the Platonic Academy; but cf. above, Sonnet II, n. 5.

XLII — *Sopra la brocca fessa*

Ben dieci volte te l'ho detto, o Tina,
fa risprangar la brocca tua di legno,
acciò che per la via non lasci il segno
quando tu vai per l'acqua la mattina.

E tu, come se fussi una bambina,
non curi quel che per tuo ben t'insegno;
ma cercheresti, se tu avessi ingegno,
di non aver da ognun la fanferina.[1]

A dir ch'e' non ti paia cosa strana
quel gocciolar, non una volta sola,
ma sempre nel tornar dalla fontana,

e che t'abbia a esser detto a ogni parola
da chiunque passa (oh, la mi par marchiana!):[2]
o Tina, tu l'hai fessa, la ti cola!

---

[1] Jeering, from *fanfara* and *fanfano*, gabber.
[2] This is a big one! possibly with ref. to the big cherries from the Marche region.

XLIII — *Sopra la siepe sturata*

La siepe, o Tina, tanto t'è cresciuta
dinanzi che il giardin tutto ritura,
e pur (cosa che pare a creder dura)
l'insalata troviam mezza pasciuta.[1]

Quest'è un segno ch'entro c'è venuta
qualche gran bestia senz'aver paura,
e ch'ha sciupato tutta la verdura,
e questa ch'è rimasta or par che puta.

O Tina mia, bisogna riturarla,
se non vuoi dalla gente aver la baia;
e s'io son buono a darti aiuto, parla!

Io gentilmente, in mo' che non si paia,
purché agio tu mi dia di rassettarla,
riturerotti tutta la callaia.[2]

---

[1] Half-grazed.
[2] Passage through a hedge, from Lat. *callis*, foot-path.

XLIV — *Sopra la bigoncia*[1]

L'uva è già ghezza[2] e sono in molle i tini,
sicché vendemmiar puossi a nostra posta,[3]
Tina, e tra noi di quel che non ci costa
far a combutta come buon vicini.

Di quel che a te darò non vo' quattrini,
e tu a quel che a me dai non por la posta:
sia del par la domanda e la risposta,
ché così s'usa tra noi contadini.

Dopo ch'e' sia svinato, com'è onesto,
s'ognun ripiglia il suo la cosa è acconcia,
la riceuta non ci va del resto.

Ma perché meco tu non stia mai broncia,
ti lascierò l'ammostatoio[4] in presto,[5]
se a me darai l'ombuto o la bigoncia.

[1] Wooden tub used to transport grapes and transfer the pressed wine from the vat to the barrel.
[2] Black, from Lat. *aegyptius*.
[3] Equivocal rhyme: as we please, but below (l. 6), with etym. duplication, it means to put at stake.
[4] Stick with a large base used to tread the grapes, denom. from *mosto*.
[5] Sync. form of *prestito*.

XLV — *Sopra l'innestare*

Tina, tu sai ch'i' ho quel mio ciliegio
acquaiolo[1] nel campo delle fosse,
il qual vorre' innestar perché più grosse
le facesse, ché quelle io l'ho in dispregio.

E non comporta quasi a corle il pregio,
ch'altro non ha di buon che le son rosse;
bisciolo[2] lo vo' pria che più ingrosse,
ché quest'hanno tra gli altri il privilegio.

Tina mia bella, non ti paia strano
di venirmi aiutar: basta che appresso
tu mi stia, e che tenga il conio[3] in mano;

ed allargando bene ben con esso
(mentr'io metto la marza)[4] vadia piano
la buccia intorno, e poi ristringa il fesso.

---

[1] Variety of cherry tree which yields early fruits with a watery pulp.
[2] Alternate form of *visciolo*, tart cherry tree.
[3] Wedge, from Lat. *cuneus*.
[4] The shoot to be grafted, from the month of March, when the grafting is generally done.

XLVI — *Sopra il lavar il bucato*

Che giova, o Tina, andar giù nel fossato
e starti coccolon[1] su quel pietrone
a stropicciare e battere il bucato,
se non adopri punto di sapone?

Lavalo meglio, perché il tuo padrone
ha gusto grande ch'e' gli sia lavato,
e quando se gli porta ripiegato,
lo guarda prima ben, poi lo ripone.

Io m'offerisco, perché la mi preme
d'aiutarti a lavar e ben'e presto,
e di far buon lavoro ho ferma speme:

prima stropiccerem le parti estreme
de' panni entrambi, e poi d'accordo al resto
faremo al fin la saponata insieme.

---

[1] To squat, with onomatopoeic ref. to the sound made by a hen.

XLVII — *Sopra il nidio*

Ieri, nel ritornar da Montisoni,[1]
calando pel burron, passai rasente
il castagneto di Cecchin del Nente,
dov'eran già le fosse dei carboni.

Quivi un nidio trovai di gazzeroni[2]
in cima a un leccio, e perché posi mente
ch'eran stati adocchiati dalla gente,
gl'ho cavati e non hanno anco i bordoni.[3]

O Tina, se tu vuoi ch'io te li dia,
vien a torteli in man. Tina, da',[4] vienne,
che pericol non c'è ch'e' volin via.

La Mea gli vedde e voglia gliene venne,
ma i' gl'ho serbati a te, speranza mia,
perché so ch'e' ti piaccion senza penne.

[1] Hill south of Florence.
[2] Magpie chicks, from *gazza*.
[3] Shafts of the early feathers.
[4] Come on, apoc. of *dai*.

XLVIII — *Sopra il far l'olio*

O Tina, i' vo' venir teco per opra
or che l'ulive tue son grosse e nere,
e starem tutto il dì con gran piacere,
tu di sotto a raccorre, i' a scuoter sopra.

E ti prometto che nessun ci scopra,
sebben l'hai grande, d'empierti il paniere;
e poi che cerco[1] avrem tutto il podere,
per trarne l'olio le porremo in opra.

Riscalderenle bene e tra noi due,
messe dove la macina le preme,
un empierà le gabbie e un merrà il bue.

Ma prima che si faccia l'olio insieme,
se la stanga è tarlata vedrai tue,
ed io vedrò se la tinella geme.

---

[1] Sync. form of *cercato*; cf. above, *Nencio alla Tina*, n. 22.

XLIX — *Sopra la testicciola*[1]

Tina, to' quella testa e que' peducci
e metti or ora un paiol d'acqua al fuoco,
e allor che bolle tuffavegli un poco,
ma gua'[2] che nel pelar tu non gli sbucci.

Fa' presto se non vuoi ch'i' mi corrucci,
friggili bene, e poi qui 'n questo loco
portali; e se mangiamgli a poco a poco,
ch'i' arrazzi[3] se le dita non ti succi!

L'agnello cotto, quando il grasso cola,
non par che dal capretto si distingua;
poi gl'è un mangiar da re la testicciuola.

Vo' che la fame a tramendue s'estingua:
a te ogni cosa vo' cacciar in gola,
perché a me basta sol l'occhio e la lingua.

---

[1] Stew made with lamb's or goat's head, often served with fried feet.
[2] Watch out, apoc. of *guarda*.
[3] I'll be blowed, denom. from *razzo*.

L — *Sopra il voltar le rene*

Gl'è com'il confettar propio una rapa,[1]
il piaggiar[2] oggigiorno una fanciulla;
faccia un, se sa che alfine e' non fa nulla,
consuma il tempo e l'opra non accapa.[3]

L'ha una gallòria,[4] s'ella se l'incapa,
che tien l'uom come il lin nella maciulla.
Or ch'io non amo e il cuor più non mi frulla,
e' mi par di star ben quanto stia un papa.

Tina, non creder più col tuo discorso
far sì ch'io torni a rivolerti bene,
ché a Modona non vo' più menar l'orso.[5]

Conosco il mancamento d'onde e' viene:
s'un per te muore e chiedeti soccorso,
tu abbassi il capo e voltigli le schiene.

---

[1] 'Like turning turnips into marmalade.'
[2] To court with flattery, probably from Lat. *plagiare*.
[3] Achieve, get to the bottom, from *capo*; cf. below, l. 5.
[4] Revelry, comp. of *gallo* and *gloria*.
[5] Pursuit which is not worth the trouble, from the use of bringing a living bear to Modena as annuity for the House of Este, which granted the lease on the woods of the Garfagnana region.

NOTE ON THE TEXT

~

The above text is based on the 1637 autograph manuscript of *La Tina* preserved at the National Library of Scotland, Edinburgh, Adv. MS 19. 3. 40. The manuscript is bound in green morocco with gilt fore-edges. In the old *Poetry Catalogue* of the Advocates Library (NLS, MS FR 190), completed around 1830, *La Tina* is recorded as '4to', but the present size is slightly smaller than octavo, measuring 199 × 140 mm. Before receiving its current binding, the manuscript must have been trimmed because it had become worn or torn, as witnessed by minor repairs to the edges, in particular to the lower corners. Date and provenance of the binding are unknown, but a *terminus a quo* is provided by the flyleaf at the beginning, which is watermarked '1814'.

Malatesti's original dedication manuscript consisted of thirty-two leaves of fine laid paper, now at fols 7–38, watermarked with a Latin cross in a pointed oval, above initials which are difficult to read (see *Introduction*, n. 92). This manuscript was bound together with additional leaves to accommodate Giuseppe Baretti's *Notizie intorno all'Autore*, at fols 3ᵛ–7ᵛ, and several annotations by Thomas Hollis at fols 3ʳ, 39ʳ, and 39ʳ/bis. On the lower margin of fol. 1ʳ there is the epigraph, in Hollis's handwriting, from Petrarch's *Triumphus Famæ*: 'Che trae l'uom dal sepolcro, e 'n vita il serba'. Fol. 2ʳ contains Antonio Francini's dedicatory stanza 'Di bella gloria amante'. The foliation is added in pencil in the top right corner of the rectos; it begins after two blank leaves and ends at fol. 39/bis (numbered 39), followed by nineteen unfoliated blank leaves. Two rough-paper leaves, respectively at the beginning and at the end, are without visible watermark and conspicuously foxed. The watermarks on the additional annotated leaves alternate between a post horn within a crowned crest, above the initials 'L V G' (Lubertus Van Gerrevink), and an unidentified monogram; the last fourteen blank leaves are watermarked with a simple fleur-de-lys.

The famous dedication to Milton, in the form of a stone-tablet inscription, is on fol. 8ʳ. On the lower part of this folio there are some handwritten marks which are difficult to decipher, but could be tentatively read as follows: the English date 'ye 2ⁿᵈ Nov 1684', the initials 'J. A.', and the signature 'TDeane' (see *Introduction*, n. 95). The dedicatory letter *Nencio alla Tina* is at fols 9ʳ–10ᵛ, followed by Malatesti's sonnets at fols 11ʳ–35ᵛ.

In the present edition, the titles of the fifty equivocations, which the author gathered in a *Tavola* at fols 36ʳ–37ʳ, are given together with the roman numerals that mark the series. There are two notable authorial variants: 'talento' instead of 'giudizio' in the dedicatory letter, fol. 9ʳ; and 'rotto' instead of 'ghiotto' in Sonnet XXIII. 13, fol. 22ᵛ. The word 'pozzo' in Sonnet XXII. 4 is a correction of 'posso' and is followed by a sign which resembles an underlined 'm'; the sigmatized form is typical of western Tuscan dialects, and it may be explained as a playful mimetic reference to Pisa, as in Sonnet II. 8. Sonnets XXXIV (*Sopra il mangiar le fave*) and XXXV (*Sopra il nibbio*) are inverted in all printed editions.

As is common practice in critical editions, I have consistently expanded abbreviations and made minor alterations — where necessary or useful to the reader — in punctuation, word division, and capitalization according to standard modern Italian usage. Tuscan spelling, however, is largely preserved. Footnotes clarify the lesser-known Tuscan idioms and local references. The obscene metaphors should be obvious to any reader, let alone to a post-Freudian mind. Relevant dictionaries are listed in the *Bibliography*, section 3. Where possible, I give in inverted commas the translation by Donald Sears, from '*La Tina*: The Country Sonnets of Malatesti as Dedicated to Mr. John Milton, English Gentleman', *Milton Studies*, 13 (1979), 284–317.

BIBLIOGRAPHY

~

1. Malatesti's Published Works

Brindis de Ciclopi (Florence: Stamperia della Stella, 1673)

Brindisi d'Antonio Malatesti e di Pietro Salvetti: con annotazioni. Dedicati all'Illustriss. Sig. Bindo Simone Peruzzi, ed. by Giuseppe Maria Bianchini and Anton Maria Biscioni (Florence: Manni, 1723)

Dialogo di un Poeta e di uno Scapigliato: Astianatte Molino, Galeazzo Titta [and other poems], in *Il Propugnatore: studi filologici, storici e bibliografici di vari socî della Commissione pe' Testi di Lingua*, 6/1 (1873), 103–12

Enimmi, ossieno Indovinelli piacevoli e galanti, finora inediti, ed. by Modesto Rastrelli (Florence: Benucci e Compp., 1782)

Il Cecco da Scandicci, mandato via contra tempo dal Podere. Alle bellissime Dame (Florence: Stamperia di S.A.S, 1666)

La compagnia di Belfiore per consolazione degli spiantati, in *Rime burlesche di eccellenti autori*, ed. by Pietro Fanfani (Florence: Le Monnier, 1856), pp. 30–32

La Sfinge: enimmi (Venice: Sarzina, 1640–1641; Florence: Stamperia di S.A.S, 1643)

Lettera familiare a Lorenzo Lippi, descrivendogli la sua vita, ed. by Giulio Piccini (Florence: Cellini e C., 1867)

Lezione su Petrarca all'Accademia degli Apatisti, in *Padova in onore di Francesco Petrarca, MCMIV*, ed. by Vincenzo Crescini, Francesco Flamini, Andrea Moschetti, and Albino Zenatti, 2 vols (Padua: Società Cooperativa Tipografica, 1904–09), II: *Miscellanea di studi critici e ricerche erudite* (1909), 74–83

Rinaldo infuriato: poema, in *Poesie piacevoli e burlesche per divertimento, e passatempo, di vari eccellenti autori*, ed. by Modesto Rastrelli, 6 vols (Yverdon [Florence: Benucci], 1782), III (canto I), IV (cantos II–III)

2. Editions of *La Tina*

La Tina: equivoci rusticali di Antonio Malatesti fiorentino, composti nella sua villa di Tajano il settembre dell'anno 1637 e da lui regalati al grande poeta inghilese Giovanni Milton (London [Venice]: Edlin [Alvisopoli], 1757 [ca. 1837])

La Tina: equivoci rusticali in cinquanta sonetti di Antonio Malatesti fiorentino, composti nella sua villa di Tajano il settembre dell'anno 1637 e da lui regalati al grande poeta inghilese Giovanni Milton (London [Florence]: A spese dell'editore [Gargini, 1859])

La Sfinge, Brindisi de' Ciclopi e La Tina, ed. by Pietro Fanfani (Milan: Corradetti, 1865)

La Sfinge: enimmi di Antonio Malatesti. Con aggiunta La Tina, ed. by Ettore Allodoli (Lanciano: Carabba, 1913)

La Tina da Castello: aggiuntavi La Geva di Alessandro Allegri, ed. by Clemente Valacca (Messina: Principato, 1914)

La Tina, ed. by Sebastiano Blancato (Milan: Il Ruscello, 1945)

La Tina (Foligno: Del Romano, 1946)

La Tina, ed. by Mirella Masieri (Rome: Salerno Editrice, 2005)

3. Dictionaries

BARETTI, GIUSEPPE, *A Dictionary of the English and Italian Languages*, 2 vols (London: Richardson, 1760)

COLUSSI, GIORGIO, *Glossario degli antichi volgari italiani* (Helsinki and Foligno: Editoriale umbra, 1982– in progress)

Dizionario letterario del lessico amoroso: metafore, eufemismi, trivialismi, ed. by Valter Boggione and Giovanni Casalegno, 2nd edn (Turin: UTET, 2000)

FANFANI, PIETRO, *Vocabolario dell'uso toscano*, 2 vols (Florence: Barbera, 1863; facsimile repr. Florence: Fotocromo Emiliana, 1976)

GIACCHI, PIRRO, *Dizionario del vernacolo fiorentino: etimologico, storico, aneddotico, artistico. Aggiunte le voci simboliche, metaforiche e syncopate dei pubblici venditori* (Florence-Rome: Bencini, 1878)

Grande Dizionario della Lingua Italiana, dir. by Salvatore Battaglia and Giorgio Bàrberi Squarotti, 21 vols (Turin: UTET, 1961–2002)

Vocabolario degli Accademici della Crusca (Venice: Alberti, 1612; facsimile repr. Florence-Varese: Era, 2008)

4. Secondary Literature

AGLIETTI, MARIO, 'Avvertenza', in Pietro Salvetti, *Rime giocose edite e inedite di un umorista fiorentino del secolo XVII* (Florence: Bertelli, 1904), pp. 1–49

ALLODOLI, ETTORE, *Giovanni Milton e l'Italia* (Prato: Vestri & Spighi, 1907)

ARBIZZONI, GUIDO, 'Poesia epica, eroicomica, satirica, burlesca. La poesia rusticale toscana. La poesia figurata', in *Storia della letteratura italiana*, dir. by Enrico Malato, 14 vols (Rome: Salerno Editrice, 1995–2004), V: *La fine del Cinquecento e il Seicento* (1997), 727–70

BELLONI, ANTONIO, *Il Seicento* (Milan: Vallardi, 1947)

BENVENUTI, EDOARDO, *Agostino Coltellini e l'Accademia degli Apatisti a Firenze nel secolo XVII* (Pistoia: Officina Tipografica Cooperativa, 1910)

BLACKBURNE, FRANCIS, *Memoirs of Thomas Hollis* (London: Nichols, 1780)

CINQUEMANI, ANTHONY M., *Glad to Go for a Feast: Milton, Buonmattei, and the Florentine Accademici* (New York: Lang, 1998)

CISTERNINO, PAOLA, 'Aspetti della poesia burlesca del Seicento: gli *Enimmi* di Antonio Malatesti', in *I Capricci di Proteo: percorsi e linguaggi del Barocco* (Atti del Convegno di Lecce, 23–26 ottobre 2000), ed. by Bruno Basile and others (Rome: Salerno Editrice, 2002), pp. 773–81

COCHRANE, ERIC, *Florence in the Forgotten Centuries, 1527–1800* (Chicago and London: University of Chicago Press, 1973)

COLTELLINI, AGOSTINO, 'Dialogo Rhytmico, seu Sonetto Etrusco tra 'l Discipulo e 'l Pedagogo', in *Endecasyllabi Fidentiani del signor Ostilio Contalgeni Accademico Apatista: parte seconda* (Florence: Massi, 1652), pp. 26–7

CONTINI, GIANFRANCO, 'La poesia rusticale come caso di bilinguismo', in *La poesia rusticana nel Rinascimento: Atti del Convegno* (Rome: Accademia Nazionale dei Lincei, 1969), pp. 43–55; now in *Ultimi esercizî ed elzeviri* (Turin: Einaudi, 1989), pp. 6–21

CORNEY, BOLTON, 'Milton and Malatesti', *Notes and Queries*, 202 (1853), 237–38

DATI, CARLO R., 'Lettera al Signor Antonio Malatesti, nella quale si discorre degli "Enimmi"', in *La Sfinge: enimmi di Antonio Malatesti*, pp. 13–17

DE FILIPPIS, MICHELE, 'Antonio Malatesti', in *The Literary Riddle in Italy in the Seventeenth Century* (Berkeley-Los Angeles: University of California Press, 1953), pp. 116–48

DELLA TORRE, ARNALDO 'Una lezione di Antonio Malatesti su Petrarca all'Accademia degli Apatisti', in *Padova in onore di Francesco Petrarca*, II, 59–74

DE MIRANDA, GIROLAMO, 'Malatesti, Antonio', in *Dizionario Biografico degli Italiani*, vol. 68 (Rome: Istituto della Enciclopedia Italiana Treccani, 2007), pp. 114–16

FANFANI, PIETRO, 'Della poesia giocosa e di Antonio Malatesti', in Malatesti, *La sfinge, I Brindisi de' Ciclopi e La Tina*, pp. v–xxxi

FERRARIO, GIULIO, 'Agli amatori dell'amena poesia', in *Poesie pastorali e rusticali, raccolte ed illustrate, con note* (Milan: Società Tipografica de' Classici Italiani, 1808), pp. iii–xxxviii

FIORETTI, BENEDETTO, *Proginnasmi poetici di Udeno Nisieli da Vernio, Accademico Apatista*, 5 vols (Florence: Pignoni, 1620–39)

GALILEI, GALILEO, *Opere*, ed. by Antonio Favaro, 20 vols (Florence: Barbèra, 1890–1909), IX: *Scritti letterari* (1899)

GILLET, JOSEPH E., 'Notes on the Language of the Rustics in the Drama of the Sixteenth Century', in *Homenaje ofrecido a Menéndez Pidal*, 3 vols (Madrid: Hernando, 1925), I, 443–53

HAAN, ESTELLE, *From Academia to Amicitia: Milton's Latin Writings and the Italian Academies* (Philadelphia: American Philosophical Society, 1998)

IMBERT, GAETANO, *La vita fiorentina nel Seicento, secondo memorie sincrone (1644–1670)* (Florence: Bemporad & Figlio, 1906)

INGHIRAMI, FRANCESCO, *Storia della Toscana, compilata ed in sette epoche distribuita*, 16 vols (Fiesole: Poligrafia Fiesolana, 1843), X: *Epoca 6: dall'anno 1530 al 1737 dopo G. Cr. Dei tempi Medicei*

KLIGER, SAMUEL, 'Milton in Italy and the Lost Malatesti Manuscript,' *Studies in Philology*, 51 (1954), 208–13

LAZZERI, ALESSANDRO, *Intellettuali e consenso nella Toscana del Seicento: l'Accademia degli Apatisti* (Milan: Giuffrè, 1983)

LILJEGREN, STEN BODVAR, 'Milton at Florence', *Neophilologus*, 43 (1959), 133–37

LIMENTANI, UBERTO, *La satira nel Seicento* (Milan: Ricciardi 1961)

LIPPI, LORENZO, *Il Malmantile racquistato: poema di Perlone Zipoli* (Finaro [Florence]: Rossi, 1676); commented edn *Il Malmantile racquistato di Perlone Zipoli, con le note di Puccio Lamoni* [Paolo Minucci], ed. by Anton Maria Biscioni, 2 vols (Florence: Moücke, 1750)

LONGHI, SILVIA, *Lusus: il capitolo burlesco nel Cinquecento* (Padova: Antenore, 1983)

MANNI, DOMENICO MARIA, 'Prefazione', in *Brindisi d'Antonio Malatesti e di Pietro Salvetti*, pp. xi–xxviiii

MARCHETTI, ITALIANO, 'Note sulla poesia rusticale', *Studi secenteschi*, 1 (1960), 61–81

MARINI, QUINTO, 'Barocco in villa: le ingegnose Arcadie del Seicento', in *I Capricci di Proteo*, pp. 333–77

MARZO, ANTONIO, *Note sulla poesia erotica del Cinquecento* (Lecce: Adriatica, 1999)

MASIERI, MIRELLA, '*La Tina, ovvero i sonetti erotici di Antonio Malatesti*', in *I Capricci di Proteo*, pp. 857–66

MAYLENDER, MICHELE, *Storia delle Accademie d'Italia*, 5 vols (Bologna: Cappelli, 1926–30), I (1926), 219–26

MERLINI, DOMENICO, *Saggio di ricerche sulla satira contro il villano* (Milan: Loescher, 1894)

NARDO, ANNA K., 'Milton and the Academic Sonnet', in *Milton in Italy: Contexts, Images, Contradictions*, ed. by Mario A. Di Cesare (Binghamton, NY: MRTS, 1991), pp. 489–503

NELLI, GIOVANNI BATTISTA C., *Saggio di storia letteraria fiorentina del secolo XVII* (Florence: Giuntini, 1759)

NERI, ACHILLE, 'All'Onorevole Sig. Direttore del Propugnatore', *Il Propugnatore*, 6/1 (1873), 90–102

NIGRO, SALVATORE SILVANO, 'Il "dilettevole stile giocoso", in lingua e in dialetto', in *Storia generale della letteratura italiana*, ed. by Nino Borsellino and Walter Pedullà, 12 vols (Milan: Motta, 1999), vol. VI: *Il secolo Barocco*, pp. 247–300

OLDCORN, ANTHONY, 'The Anti-Classicist Tradition: Parody, Satire, Burlesque', in *CHIL*, pp. 268–76

PREZZINER, GIOVANNI, *Storia del pubblico studio e delle società scientifiche e letterarie di Firenze*, 2 vols (Florence: Carli, 1810)

RASTRELLI, MODESTO, 'Breve notizia intorno alla vita d'Antonio Malatesti Fiorentino', in *Enimmi, ossieno Indovinelli*, pp. 5–15

REDI, FRANCESCO, *Bacco in Toscana: ditirambo* (Florence: Matini, 1685); now ed. by Giovanni Cipriani and Ugo Centurioni (Bergamo: Veronelli, 1995)

RICHARDSON, BRIAN, '"Recitato e cantato": the Oral Diffusion of Lyric Poetry in Sixteenth-Century Italy', in *Theatre, Opera, and Performance in Italy from the Fifteenth Century to the Present: Essays in Honour of Richard Andrews*, ed. by Brian Richardson, Simon Gilson, and Catherine Keen (Egham: Society for Italian Studies, 2004), pp. 67–82

ROMEI, DANILO, 'Il linguaggio dell'equivoco', in *Da Leone X a Clemente VII. Scrittori toscani nella Roma dei papati medicei (1513–1534)* (Manziana: Vecchiarelli, 2007), pp. 243–66

SAMPSON, LISA, *Pastoral drama in Early Modern Italy: The Making of a New Genre* (London: Legenda, 2006)

SEARS, DONALD, '*La Tina*: The Country Sonnets of Malatesti as Dedicated to Mr. John Milton, English Gentleman', *Milton Studies*, 13 (1979), 275–83

SINGER, SAMUEL W., 'Milton and Malatesti', *Notes and Queries*, 204 (1853), 295–96

STERZI, MARIO, 'Jacopo Cicognini', *Giornale storico e letterario della Liguria*, 3 (1902), 289–338

TESAURO, EMANUELE, 'Metafora terza: di equivoco', in *Il Cannocchiale Aristotelico: o sia Idea dell'Arguta et Ingeniosa Elocutione che serve a tutta l'Arte Oratoria,*

Lapidaria, et Simbolica, Esaminata co' Principij del Divino Aristotele (Turin: Zavatta, 1670), pp. 365–96

TOSCAN, JEAN, *Le Carnaval du langage: le lexique érotique des poètes de l'équivoque de Burchiello à Marino (XVᵉ–XVIIᵉ siècles)*, 4 vols (Lille: Presses Universitaires, 1981)

VALACCA, CLEMENTE, 'Prefazione', in Antonio Malatesti, *La Tina da Castello: aggiuntavi La Geva di Alessandro Allegri* (Messina: Principato, 1914), pp. 1–7

VARCHI, BENEDETTO, *L'Hercolano* (1570), ed. by Antonio Sorella, 2 vols (Pescara: Libreria dell'Università Editrice, 1995)

VILLANI, NICOLA, *Ragionamento dello Accademico Aldeano sopra la poesia giocosa de' Greci, de' Latini, e de' Toscani: con alcune poesie piacevoli del medesimo autore* (Venice: Pinelli, 1634)

YATES, FRANCES A., 'The Italian Academies', in *Collected Essays*, 3 vols (London: Routledge, 1982–84), II: *Renaissance and Reform: The Italian Contribution* (1983), 6–29

MHRA Critical Texts

This series aims to provide affordable critical editions of lesser-known literary texts that are not in print or are difficult to obtain. The texts will be taken from the following languages: English, French, German, Italian, Portuguese, Russian, and Spanish. Titles will be selected by members of the distinguished Editorial Board and edited by leading academics. The aim is to produce scholarly editions rather than teaching texts, but the potential for crossover to under-graduate reading lists is recognized. The books will appeal both to academic libraries and individual scholars.

Malcolm Cook
Chairman, Editorial Board

Editorial Board

www.criticaltexts.mhra.org.uk

Lightning Source UK Ltd.
Milton Keynes UK
UKOW04f2158080414

229650UK00001B/61/P